Country Quilts &
Soft Furnishings

Country Quilts & Soft Furnishings

Cheryl Fall

 Sterling Publishing Co., Inc. New York

Library of Congress Cataloging-in-Publication Data

Fall, Cheryl C.
    Country quilts & soft furnishings / Cheryl Fall; photography by
Jay Turner.
      p. cm.
    Includes index.
    ISBN 0-8069-0433-X
    1. Quilting—Patterns. 2. Appliqué—Patterns. 3. House
furnishings. 4. Interior decoration. I. Turner, Jay. II. Title.
III. Title: Country quilts and soft furnishings.
TT835.F335   1994
746.46—dc20   93-48771
                                           CIP

10 9 8 7 6 5 4 3 2 1

Published by Sterling Publishing Company, Inc.
387 Park Avenue South, New York, N.Y. 10016
© 1994 by Cheryl Fall
Distributed in Canada by Sterling Publishing
℅ Canadian Manda Group, P.O. Box 920, Station U
Toronto, Ontario, Canada M8Z 5P9
Distributed in Great Britain and Europe by Cassell PLC
Villiers House, 41/47 Strand, London WC2N 5JE, England
Distributed in Australia by Capricorn Link (Australia) Pty Ltd.
P.O. Box 6651, Baulkham Hills, Business Centre, NSW 2153, Australia
Printed in China.
All rights reserved

Sterling ISBN 0-8069-0433X

Cover photograph by Nancy Palubniak.

Text photos: pages 28, 41, 45, 53, 57, 64, 70, 78, 85, 94, 102,
115, 126 by Jay Turner, Vancouver, Washington; pages 26, 29,
47, 56, 58, 72, 87, 97, 111, 119, 131, 132 by Nancy Palubniak,
New York City.

Edited by Isabel Stein.

Contents

Preface

Making things to decorate your home with is both exciting and satisfying. You will always feel a great sense of pride when someone admires something in your home that you have made yourself. A room featuring handmade accents is warm and inviting. It's a place full of personality and a place to linger awhile!

The projects in this book are both fun and easy. Even those projects that look more involved are easy to make when you follow our detailed directions, as we guide you through every step with easy-to-understand instructions and detailed diagrams.

Choosing the fabrics for the projects is part of the fun of making them! You can set a mood with the colors and styles of fabrics you choose, whether it be country style, Victorian or contemporary. A dark corner can be perked up with something as simple as a brightly colored pillow or floor cloth. A dull kitchen can be made warm and inviting with new tabletop accessories, such as tea cozies and place mats.

You can customize any of these projects according to your own taste and preferences, or to those of a friend or relative; any of these projects would also make a lovely gift for someone special.

Happy stitching!

Acknowledgments

To Mom and Dad: what would I do without you! Thanks for having faith in me! And to my husband, Tony—your patience and support are incredible! You've helped me more than you can ever imagine.

A special thank you to the following manufacturers and individuals who shared their products and knowledge: Coats & Clark, Singer Sewing Machine Company, Handler Textile Corporation, V.I.P. Fabrics, C.M. Offray & Sons, Stearns Technical Textiles Corp./ Mountain Mist, Wimpole Street Creations, and St. Louis Trimming Company.

Supplies, Tools, and Techniques

Necessary Supplies

Before you begin any of the projects in this book, read through the introductory chapters on supplies, tools, and techniques, and gather all of them together.

1. Fabric Choice and Preparation

The fabrics I recommend are all 100% cotton, 44 to 45 inches wide. I prefer to use cotton fabrics because they are very durable and are easy to handle during stitching. Synthetics and blends tend to slip while you are stitching, and they fray easily.

Prewash and press all of the fabrics before cutting to avoid shrinkage of the projects you intend to wash later. Prewashing also removes the factory sizing (stiffening agent) and makes the fabric easier to stitch. Always wash like colors separately and make sure that none of the fabrics "bleeds" or "crocks" (isn't colorfast). If a fabric continues to bleed, there's a pretty good chance it will always do so, and it may stain its neighbors in your project. Replace it with another fabric. Tumble-dry the fabrics in an automatic dryer; for best results, remove them from the dryer just before they are completely dry and press them to complete the drying process, making sure you keep the fabric on grain (see grainline diagram, Figure 1).

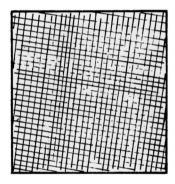

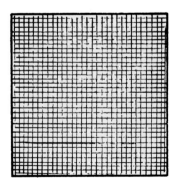

1. *Two fabric swatches. **a** is off-grain, as can be seen by the fabric weave lines that are at an angle to the edges of the swatch. **b** is correct; the grainlines are parallel to the edges of the swatch.*

TIP: If a pattern calls for a scrap piece of fabric and you are unsure if your scrap-basket fabric has been washed yet, you can wash it easily, without losing it in your washer, by swishing it around in a sink with hot sudsy water and rinsing it thoroughly. Wring the excess water from the piece and lay it flat to dry, straightening the grain as you lay it out.

2. Thread

I prefer to use all-purpose sewing thread in my projects. It is readily available and comes in a multitude of colors, making it easy to find a perfect match to your fabrics. My favorite thread is a cotton-wrapped polyester, which is available worldwide. If you prefer, you may also use 100% cotton thread, although you will not have as wide a range of colors to choose from. Also, you run the risk of your thread shrinking, while your preshrunk fabrics remain stable.

3. Batting and Fleece

The projects in this book use traditional-weight polyester quilt batting or polyester fleece. Quilt batting comes in a multitude of weights, such as "traditional," "low-loft," and "high-loft." ("Loft" means resilience of textile fibre.) The fibre content of batting may be polyester, cotton, or a poly–cotton blend. If you purchase a cotton or a blend, read the package carefully as some of them require special handling or washing before you use them. Also, check the package to see if the manufacturer makes quilting recommendations; some battings perform best when the quilting stitches are closely spaced. In general, polyester battings can be quilted very loosely with wide spaces between the stitching lines, while cottons need to be quilted with closely spaced stitches to keep the batting from shifting during use or when you wash the quilt.

Quilt batting is sold either by the bag, with precut pieces in various sizes, or from a large bolt in fabric stores. If you buy batting in a fabric store, be sure to tell the salesperson you want the kind for quilting, rather than upholstery batting.

Fleece is a denser form of polyester batting; it performs best in projects that may need some extra body, such as place mats, tea cozies, or wall hangings. It is sold by the yard off bolts at the fabric stores. If you prefer, you may substitute batting for fleece in the projects given here.

TIP: Do not purchase a high-loft or "fat" batting for any of the projects in this book. These are meant for tied quilts and comforters and are extremely thick. High-loft battings are not recommended for hand or machine quilting.

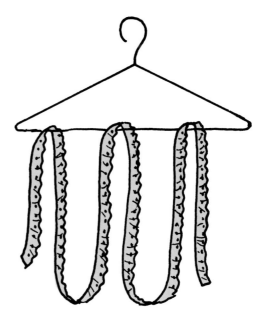

2. Lace, drying on a plastic hanger.

4. Lace and Trim

Choose lace or trim that are good quality; those tables full of "bargain" laces aren't always the bargain they appear to be. Shop wisely (this applies to fabrics as well). Prewash your lace and trim by swishing them in a sink of hot sudsy water and rinsing them thoroughly. Hang them from a plastic hanger to dry (Figure 2). Prepackaged binding generally does not require prewashing, as the manufacturer does this for you; also, in prewashing you run the risk of stretching the bias edges or losing its prefolded divisions.

5. Fusible Transfer Webbing

Fusible transfer webbing is used to bond fabric pieces to be appliquéd to the base fabric before they are machine-appliquéd in place, so that they won't move during sewing.

When the project calls for "fusible transfer webbing," use a paper-backed webbing. This can go by many brand names. To use the fusible transfer webbing, first trace a reversed image of the pattern piece onto the paper side of the webbing. Fuse the rough side of the webbing to the wrong side of your appliqué fabric (see Figure 3) and cut out the pattern piece plus webbing: this will become an appliqué. Appliqué pieces don't have to be aligned in any way with the straight grain of the fabric when you cut them. To fuse the appliqué to your base fabric, remove the paper backing, position the appliqué on the right side of the base fabric, and fuse them with a hot iron, according to the webbing manufacturer's direction.

A few tips for successful fusing follow.

• Always press and lift your iron, do not slide it from place to place on the fabric.

• When you attach the appliqué to the base fabric, remember to put the rough (fusible) side of the appliqué face-down.

• Always check the bond between webbing and fabric before attempting to remove the

paper backing; press the webbing and fabric again, if necessary, to get a good bond.

6. Stabilizer

When making a project that requires machine appliqué, always use a stabilizer; it may be purchased by the yard, or you can use lightweight typing paper. This will prevent the fabric from shifting while it is under the needle; prevent puckers in the area where the appliqué meets the base fabric; and provide smooth, evenly filled, finished appliqué edges.

To use stabilizer, attach a piece of it that is slightly larger than the appliqué piece to the wrong side of the base fabric with straight pins; if you're appliquéing a whole block, cut a piece of stabilizer the size of the block and pin it to the wrong side of the block. When you have completed stitching the appliqué, simply remove the stabilizer by tearing it from the wrong side of the fabric piece.

Some stabilizers are water-soluble. They may be used as directed above, but are removed with water. For all practical purposes, the tear-away variety of stabilizer was used in the model projects in this book.

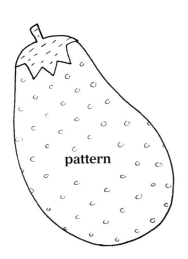

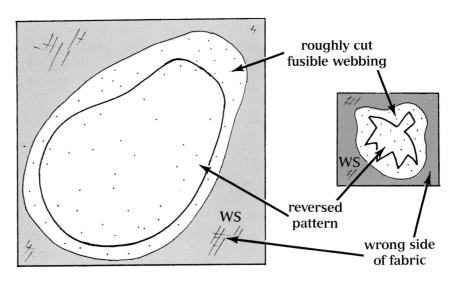

3. A reversed pattern piece, traced onto paper side of fusible webbing, which was then fused onto the back of a piece of fabric.

Tools and Tips

You'll need various tools to make your projects. If you already sew, you may have most of them on hand already.

1. Sewing Machine

Your sewing machine should be kept in good order. It is a piece of machinery, much like your car—and you wouldn't neglect your car, would you?

It needs to be cleaned regularly to remove lint and dust that could clog the feed dogs or damage the gears. It must be oiled to keep it running smoothly—not to mention quietly. If your machine is noisy, you can bet it needs oiling pronto! Consult the owner's manual of your sewing machine regarding where and how often to oil it.

Also, make sure you change your needle REGULARLY! If you still have the original needle that was in your machine 20 years ago, honey, you'll be surprised what a new needle can do for you! If your machine is in good working order, but it tends to skip stitches, pucker fabric, or pull the bobbin thread to the surface, you need to change your needle, as it has either gotten very dull or has a burr that is catching things it shouldn't.

If changing your needle doesn't help, you may need to take your machine in for a profes-sional tune-up to have the tension readjusted (if you're unable to do this yourself), or for new parts.

2. Scissors

Always have a nice, sharp pair of scissors, marked with a tag that states: FOR FABRIC ONLY. Do not cut paper or other objects with this pair of scissors; using them on anything but fabric will dull them very quickly. If you have children, mark it with a skull and crossbones—anything to keep them from using them—or hide them, as I have to do to keep my 2 children from using them! Some quilters put out other scissors for their children to use so they'll leave the fabric scissors alone.

If your scissors hurt your hands while you are cutting, they probably need to be sharpened, but sometimes oiling the scissor joint with a lubricant helps. You will need a general-use scissors for cutting patterns and templates out of paper or cardboard also.

3. Rotary Cutter and Cutting Mat

Rotary cutters have a circular blade in a handle; they look somewhat like pizza cutters. The blades are replaceable. As with scissors, make sure the blade is sharp. Test it on scrap before starting a project. Insert a new blade if the cutter skips areas while you are cutting. A rotary cutter is supposed to save time, not make more work for you when you have to make a second pass over a cut line because the blade was skipping! Rotary cutters are available in several sizes. I prefer to use one of the large-size rotary cutters, as the small ones just don't feel as stable in my hand. Don't use a rotary cutter on an unprotected table as it will (a) dull the blade quickly and (b) ruin the table. Use a self-healing plastic cutting mat, the larger the better, to cut on; they are sold at quilting supply shops. Use a wide see-through ruler for cutting (a 6″ × 24″ size is ideal) and ALWAYS cut away from you.

Be very careful with a rotary cutter; the blades are very sharp. Always keep it out of the reach of little ones (and, sometimes, curious husbands). Some rotary cutters have a feature that automatically retracts the blade when the cutter is lifted from the board; on others, you must manually retract the blade. Always use the safety features.

4. Marking Pens and Pencils

Always use water-soluble pens and pencils to mark appliqué placement, quilting lines, embroidery lines, etc. on fabric. If in doubt, test the pen or pencil by writing on a piece of fabric and washing it to be sure it washes out. Never use a #2 graphite pencil to mark fabric. Also, don't sharpen any pencil to a sharp point, as you could accidentally tear fibres in the fabric while marking it. Tap the pencil end on your table to blunt the point slightly.

5. Seam Ripper

If you sew clothing, you may already have one of these. Its sharp, curved blade can rapidly cut faulty stitches. Keep it handy. It's better to rip and restitch than to have a crooked quilt. As with any sharp tool, keep it out of the reach of small children.

6. Quilting Hoops and Frames

Hoops and frames are used for hand-quilting.

Quilting hoops are like embroidery hoops, only larger. The are available in several sizes and variations. A hoop or frame will keep your work taut as you quilt, which helps avoid puckering of the backing or top. For very large projects, a quilting frame is helpful and performs the same function. Quilting frames may be homemade or purchased, and come in a variety of sizes and styles.

7. Other Useful Items

Below is a list of other tools and supplies you'll probably need:

- Sewing machine needles (size 9 or 11 universal point for appliqué work and piecing)
- Straight pins
- Tracing paper
- Graph paper or other gridded paper for enlarging patterns
- Cardboard or plastic for cutting templates of patterns
- Thimbles for hand-sewing and quilting
- Embroidery thread for hand embroidery (see individual projects for colors)
- Needles for both hand sewing and machine sewing, including crewel embroidery needles, sharps, and betweens (short needles of sizes 5 to 11, used for hand quilting)
- A heavy plastic ruler
- A pen with waterproof ink for tracing designs on paper or cardboard
- See-through 45°–45°–90° triangle (12-inch size is good).
- Masking tape to make identifying tags for parts of quilts, etc., before they are assembled.
- An iron

Consult the materials list of the project on which you will be working for any other necessities.

Basic Techniques

1. Symbols and Abbreviations

The following symbols and abbreviations are used throughout the book:

- RS right side of fabric

- WS wrong side of fabric

- ↕ place on grainline or parallel to the finished edge of the fabric (the selvage)

2. Enlarging a Grid Pattern

Some patterns in this book are given in reduced form—for example, the apron pattern on page 109. They are given with grid marks around them and a caption indicating what size the grid units represent.

To enlarge a grid pattern to the required size (Figure 4), trace the entire pattern plus grid from the book page onto a piece of paper. Connect the intersecting grid lines with a pencil, forming a series of squares over the drawing. Label the lines vertically and horizontally. Read the caption to find out what size each square represents. Next, draw an enlarged grid, on a large piece of paper; make it with the same number of squares as the small pattern, and to the

required scale—for example, if the grid pattern says "one square equals 1″ × 1″," make the enlarged grid of one-inch squares. Label the lines on the enlarged pattern grid exactly as on the small pattern grid. Make a dot on the enlarged grid wherever the pattern line intersects a grid line. Place a second group of dots between the first group of dots by eye. Connect the dots to form the full-size pattern.

3. Machine Piecing

The pieced projects in this book utilize rotary cutting methods, which combine several cutting and sewing steps into one easy step. There are detailed directions and diagrams for each individual project. However, there are a few general things to keep in mind for all projects:

- All the projects use ¼-inch seam allowances; these seam allowances are included in all the given measurements and pattern pieces, unless otherwise noted.

- Always use a neutral thread when piecing the projects, preferably one that matches the lightest fabric in the project.

- Use an exact ¼-inch seam allowance. If you are unsure of the seam allowance on your machine, measure ¼-inch from the right of

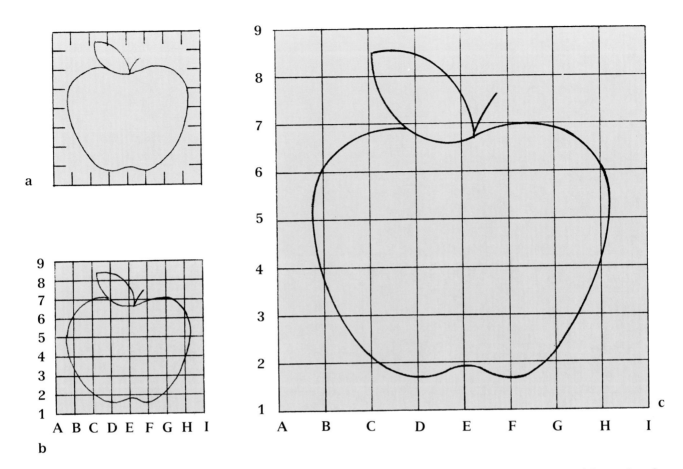

4. *Enlarging a pattern.* ***a:*** *Trace the pattern plus its grid out of the book.* ***b:*** *Connect the tick marks of the grid to form boxes over the drawing. Label the lines with letters and numbers, as shown.* ***c:*** *On a sheet of paper draw a grid of boxes of enlarged size (as indicated in the pattern's scale). Make the same number of boxes across and down as in the small drawing, and label them the same way. (Or used gridded paper if you have it.) Then put dots at each intersection on the large drawing where a pattern line intersects the grid. Connect the dots to form the enlarged pattern.*

the needle as it is in its center position with an accurate ruler. Mark this distance with a piece of masking tape on the throat plate of the machine. The stitch length should be between 10 and 12 stitches per inch for piecing.

• To save time, chain-piece (see Figure 5). Align the pieces to be joined with the right sides of fabric facing in. Stitch the first seam, then butt the next pair of pieces to be joined against the first unit stitched and continue to stitch without cutting the thread between them. When all of the same-sized units have been stitched, clip them apart and press them, as directed below.

4. Pressing

Get into the habit of pressing your pieces after stitching. To ensure accuracy, always stitch and press. After stitching a unit together, press the unit BEFORE opening it to set the seam. Then open the unit and press it. Don't use steam when you press unassembled quilt pieces, as it may cause them to stretch or warp. Always try to press the seam allowances towards the darker fabric; this will avoid the seam allowance of a darker fabric showing through a lighter piece (see Figure 6a). In some cases, such as where several seams meet, press seam allowances in opposite directions (see Figure 6b) to distribute the bulk so the unit will lie flat when completed.

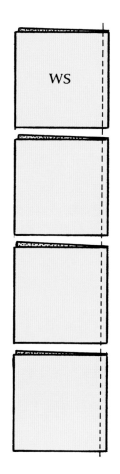

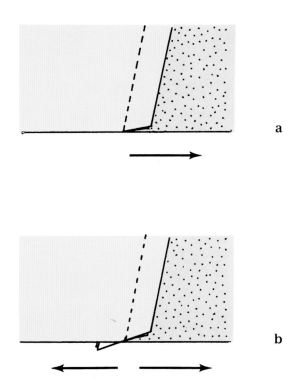

*6. Pressing seam allowances. **a**: When only a single seam allowance unit (two layers of fabric) is involved, press both layers towards the darker fabric. **b**: Where two seam allowance units meet, press each unit in an opposite direction, to distribute the bulk.*

5. Chain-piecing saves time. Here, four units of two squares each are joined to each other without breaking the thread in between; they are cut apart later.

TIP: Don't use an iron with an automatic shut-off. You'll be constantly fiddling with it if you plan to sew for any length of time. Also, an iron with a pointed sole plate can be very handy for pressing corners and small items.

5. Appliqué Basics

An appliqué is a cutout decoration of fabric that is laid on and sewn to a larger piece of fabric. Before cutting out any appliqué pieces, trace the entire block design to be appliquéd onto the base fabric in the correct place, using a water-soluble marking pencil. These tracings will be your placement lines for the appliqués. Also transfer any embroidery markings at this time.

Machine Appliqué

After fusing the appliqué pieces to your base fabric (see the section on fusible transfer webbing above), back the base fabric in the area behind the appliqué with tear-away stabilizer. Set the machine to a medium-width satin stitch, and thread it with a thread that matches the first appliqué piece. Change the top thread to match each successive appliqué piece. Use a neutral thread in the bobbin.

TIP: Stitch a test sample to make sure your satin stitch is smooth and that none of the bobbin thread is pulled to the top side of your work. If this happens, you may need to loosen the upper tension of your machine slightly. If loosening the tension does not eliminate the problem, you may need to change your needle. Use a size 9 or 11 universal point needle.

When you stitch, the satin stitch should completely cover the raw edge of the appliqué

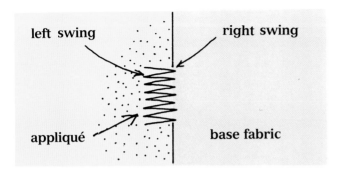

7. *The anatomy of a satin stitch. On the right swing, the thread should completely cover the raw edge of the appliqué.*

shape without extending too far into the background fabric (see Figure 7). Turn right-angled corners by stopping the needle at the point of the appliqué and pivoting the work around to the next side (see Figure 8 for pivot points). Continue to appliqué on the next side of the appliqué you pivot.

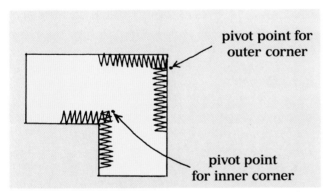

8. *Turning right-angled corners on an appliqué. Stop sewing at the pivot point, turn the work, and proceed with satin-stitching.*

If the piece comes to a tapered point (Figure 9), narrow the width of your satin stitch as you approach the point. Place the needle in the base fabric and turn the appliqué piece to stitch the next side; continue stitching, gradually widening the width of the stitch until you return to your original stitch width. To stitch a curved piece, you will need to pivot the work as you stitch to get a nice, smooth curve. To do this on an outside curve, stop the needle in the base fabric and turn the piece just slightly. To stitch an

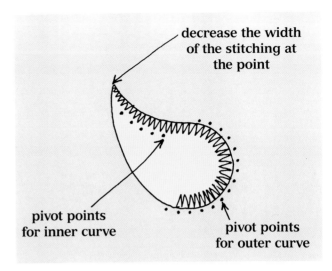

9. *Appliqué on a curved shape. Decrease the width of the satin stitch as you approach the point; stop stitching at the narrowest part and pivot the fabric; continue to satin-stitch the next side, gradually increasing the width of the satin stitch to its previous width.*

inside curve, stop the needle in the appliqué and turn the piece slightly. Repeat the pivoting process frequently (see Figure 9).

Hand Appliqué

To appliqué by hand, trace the reversed pattern shape onto the wrong side of the fabric out of which you're going to cut the appliqué piece. Cut out the appliqué shape, ADDING A ¼-INCH SEAM ALLOWANCE ALL AROUND AS YOU CUT. Turn the seam allowances of each appliqué piece to the wrong side of the piece and secure the seam allowances to the back side of the piece with hand basting (Figure 10). Press each appliqué piece.

To prepare a circle for appliqué, cut a circle template from heavy paper that is the exact size of the finished appliqué (without seam allowances). Cut a circle of fabric slightly larger than the paper template (about ¼-inch larger all around). Place the template against the wrong side of the fabric circle and gather the fabric circle to the template by hand with running stitches (Figure 11). Press the gathered circle and let it cool. Remove the paper template before stitching the circle to the base fabric.

Stitch the appliqué pieces to the base fabric using tiny, invisible hand stitches with thread that matches each appliqué piece (Figure 12).

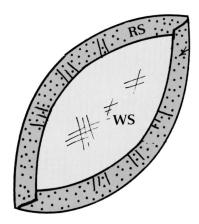

10. *Back view of a fabric piece being prepared for hand appliqué; ¼-inch seam allowances have been turned under to the wrong side of fabric, and will be secured with hand basting.*

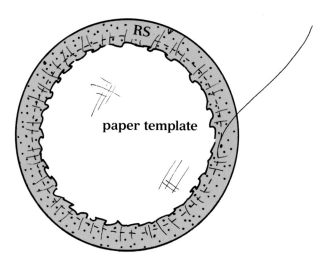

11. *Back view of a fabric circle being prepared for hand appliqué. Seam allowance of circle has been turned over a paper template and secured for pressing with gathered hand-basting stitches. Remove the paper template before attaching the appliqué.*

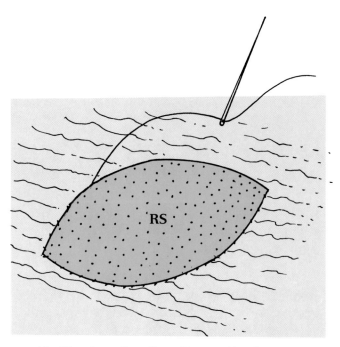

12. *Hand-appliquéing. The appliqué piece is attached with small, hidden stitches.*

6. Applying Piping and Lace

It is very easy to apply piping and lace properly. To apply either on a straight edge, simply lay the raw edges of the piping or lace along the raw edge of the right side of the fabric and baste it in place with basting stitches ¼-inch in from raw edges. When you arrive at the corner, take a small clip out of the seam allowance of the pip-

ing or lace, starting to clip ¼-inch from the corner of the fabric (see Figure 13a). Do not clip through the line of stitching on the piping or the lace! Clip up to it, but not through it. Continue basting the piping along the next edge.

To pipe or attach lace to a curved edge, clip into the seam allowance of the piping or lace near the curve at regular intervals to make the piping or lace lie flat (usually every ¼-inch to every ½-inch is sufficient). Baste the piping or lace in place ¼-inch from the raw edge (see Figure 13b).

7. Basting

A quilt may be thought of as a fabric sandwich (Figure 14). The top layer is the quilt top. The "filling" of the sandwich is the batting. The bottom layer is the quilt back, a piece of cotton fabric of whatever color or pattern you feel harmonizes well with the quilt top. Before you can hand- or machine-quilt, which unites the layers permanently, you need to join them temporarily by basting, either by machine or by hand (Figure 15).

Depending on the size of the project, you may be able to baste it on a tabletop (protected with cardboard or some other material), or on

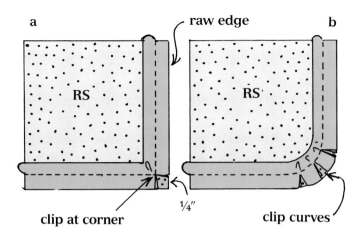

13. *Applying piping. The raw edge is aligned with the raw edge of the piece to be piped, and basted ¼-inch in from the edge. Clips are made for turning corners (a) on right angles and (b) on curves.*

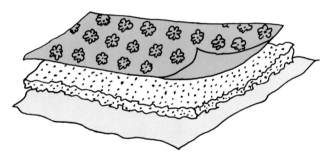

14. *Anatomy of a quilt: quilt top, batting, and quilt back.*

the floor or carpet. The basic idea is to smooth out and secure all three layers together so that you can quilt them. The quilt's backing, smoothed out but not stretched out of its actual size, should be taped face-down to your work surface, or pinned if you are working on a carpeted floor. Take the batting out of its envelope if it is folded up and unroll it if it's rolled up so that it can expand for about ½-hour before you try to baste it. Then gently spread it out, centered on the quilt back. Cut the batting and backing about 2″ larger on each side than the quilt top; you can always trim the excess off later if it's not needed. Last, center the quilt top, face-up, over the batting. Anchor all 3 layers with tape or pins to keep them from slipping while you baste. Use a color

of thread that shows up well and a long "sharp" needle if you are hand basting. For machine-basting, use a long stitch, also with contrasting colored thread. Work from the center of the quilt out to the edges and corners. Baste through all three layers, starting each new thread in the center. Be sure there are no bumps or folds. You can also go around from the center out in a spiderweb pattern. Last, run a layer of basting stitches around the outer edges of the quilt.

8. Quilting

Quilting joins the pieced and/or appliquéd quilt top, batting, and backing together securely; it also is an opportunity to add additional design elements to enrich the appearance of your project. As mentioned earlier, the actual distance that you can leave between quilting lines is determined not only by how it will look but also by the type of batting you use—cotton batting tends to sag if not quilted with lines that are closer together than those needed for polyester batting. Check the instructions on the batting you have purchased before you plan a quilting pattern. The model projects in this book all have

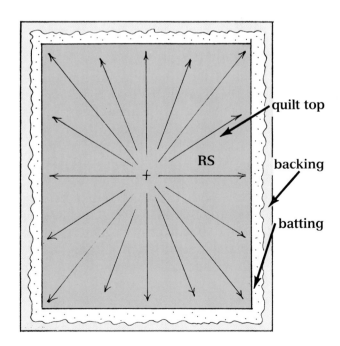

15. *Basting the quilt layers, preparatory to quilting.*

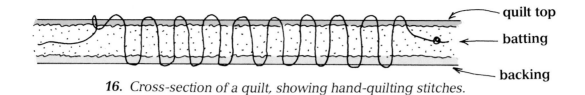

16. Cross-section of a quilt, showing hand-quilting stitches.

been machine-quilted. You may choose to hand-quilt your projects if you wish, however. Instructions for both techniques are given below. Some quilting patterns are given at the back of the book.

Hand Quilting

First assemble the three layers of the quilt as directed in the basting instructions and baste them together to secure them. Except for very small projects, you'll quilt more easily and your work will probably look better if you secure your work in a quilting hoop or, for large projects like a bed quilt, in a quilting frame (see the "Tools and Tips" chapter for more information on these). To start quilting, take a length of hand-quilting thread (about 18 inches is a good size) in the color you choose and thread it through a "between" needle (a short, thin needle of size 5 to 11). Tie a single knot in the long end of the thread. Starting at the quilt top and going down into the batting and up again, pull the thread through the top of the fabric and into the batting; push the knot through the quilt top with your fingernail, if necessary. Secure it with a quilting stitch, a short running stitch that goes through all three layers of the quilt and then comes up again close to the first stitch (see Figure 16). Experienced quilters may make as many as 10–12 stitches to the inch; beginners probably will make 4–5 to the inch. When you push the needle through the fabric, protect the third finger of your sewing hand, which remains on top of the quilt, with a thimble. Special quilter's thimbles are designed with an extra metal ridge on top to keep the needle from sliding off the thimble. The second hand remains under the quilt to receive and push the needle up again. You can protect the index finger of your second hand by wrapping a piece of adhesive tape around it or by using a leather finger guard, available in quilt shops. Quilt in whatever pattern you desire; for the projects in this book, it's

recommended you quilt around appliqué shapes and along seam lines, ¼-inch from all seam lines, and along any marked lines you choose to include.

Machine Quilting

First, assemble the three layers and baste them together, as explained in the basting section. For best results when machine-quilting, use a "walking" or "even-feed" foot on your sewing machine, available for most machines through your sewing machine dealer. Such a foot feeds the top and bottom layers of the quilt evenly, so that you will not have the puckering on the top side of the quilt that normally occurs when you use a standard machine foot. You may also choose to quilt "free-motion." To do this, drop the feed dogs or set the feed dogs in the darning position. Use a darning or spring foot in the machine (see the owner's manual of your sewing machine for more information).

Stitch along areas described in the hand-quilting section above, using thread to match the backing fabric in the bobbin, with clear nylon monofilament or a neutral-colored all-purpose thread threaded through the machine.

9. Making and Applying the Quilt Binding

The bindings I used in most of the projects are prepackaged and are marketed as "extra-wide double fold." The finished width of the binding after it is stitched to the quilt is ½-inch. This means that it was 2 inches wide before it was folded. You can make your own bias binding by cutting strips of fabric on the bias and stitching them together at the ends. This gives you a much greater choice of fabrics for binding. Calculate the perimeter of the quilt to be bound, and then cut strips that will give you a total length several inches longer, for good measure (see Figure 17).

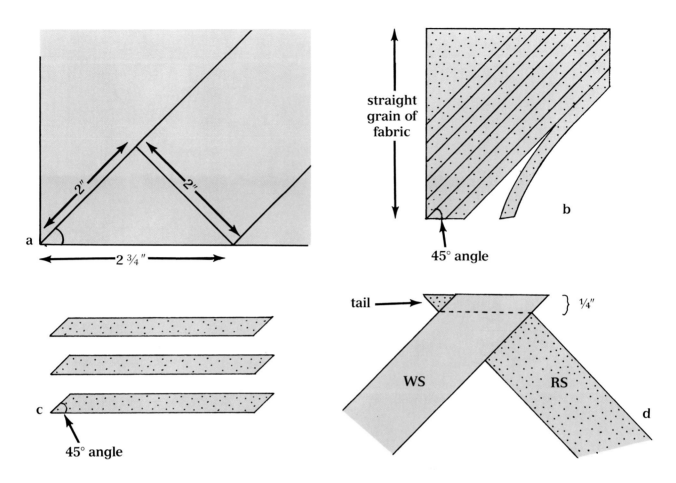

17. *Making bias binding.* **a:** *Measure and cut bias strips at a 45° angle to the crosswise grain of fabric. To get 2" wide strips you need to measure off 2¾"-long (7 cm) segments on the cross-wise line.* **b.** *Measure and cut as many strips as you need.* **c.** *The individual strips before joining.* **d.** *Join strips by sewing them together as shown, with ¼" seam allowances.*

With a ¼-inch seam allowance, stitch the ends of the bias strips together as shown in Figure 17d, slightly off center, so that the tails extend beyond the strip. When they are opened out, the edges of the joined pieces should line up exactly. Trim off the excess "tails" at each joining.

When you have finished stitching the strips together, make a fold down the center of the length of the bias strip and press it. Open the strip out again. Next, fold the sides of the strips to the center (see Figure 18a). Third, fold the tape again along the center crease and press it. The side view of the completed bias binding should look like Figure 18c.

To apply (stitch) the binding to the edges of the quilt, unfold the binding and place one raw edge against the raw edge on the quilt front with right sides of fabric facing, aligning edges. Stitch along the crease of the binding, which will be ½-inch from the edge for extra-wide binding (Figure 19a). When you get to the corner, to turn the corner of the quilt with a nice mitre, stitch to within ½-inch of the corner and cut the thread. Then, fold the bias tape upwards, aligning its edge with the edge of the next side of the quilt (Figure 19b). It will form a little triangle at the corner. Then fold the bias tape downwards, en-closing the resulting triangle, and having the top fold aligned with the first edge you stitched (Figure 19c). Continue all the way around the quilt top in the same manner.

After you have finished stitching the binding to the front of the quilt, fold the loose long edge of the binding to the back side of the quilt,

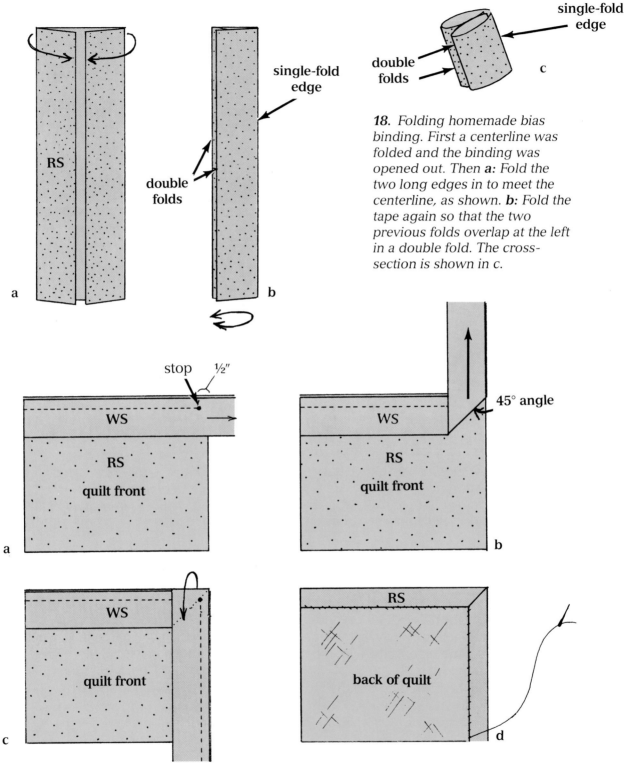

18. *Folding homemade bias binding. First a centerline was folded and the binding was opened out. Then **a:** Fold the two long edges in to meet the centerline, as shown. **b:** Fold the tape again so that the two previous folds overlap at the left in a double fold. The cross-section is shown in c.*

19. *Applying bias binding. **a:** Stitch up to ½-inch (for extra-wide binding) from the first corner, with raw edges aligned and right sides of material facing; then stop and cut the thread. **b:** Fold the bias strip up at a 45° angle. **c:** Fold the bias strip down, with the top fold aligned with the first raw edge. **d:** After turning the unattached long raw edge of the bias binding over to the quilt back, slipstitch it in place with a ½-inch seam allowance turned under.*

turning under ½-inch of raw edge on the back, and hand-stitch it in place (Figure 19d).

10. Clipping Curves and Corners

This is an often overlooked step in many sewing projects, but it does have an important purpose. Clipping the seam allowances of the curves reduces the bulk along the edges of a project when the item is turned right-side out. Also, it helps the project lie properly, instead of curling where it shouldn't. Figure 20a shows how small triangular pieces are clipped from a curved seam allowance. Be careful not to clip the stitching when you do this, however.

Clipping the excess seam allowance at the corners of a rectangular project reduces the bulk at the corners, and will make your corners appear nice and pointed, instead of looking rounded (Figure 20b).

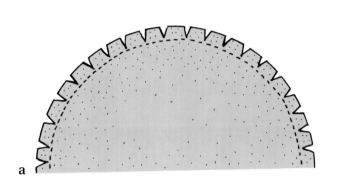

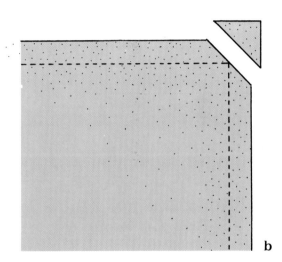

*20. Clipping the seam allowances of **a**, a curved unit, and **b**, a rectangular unit, will help to ensure a flat quilt surface once they are turned.*

The Projects

Spinning Flowers Bed Quilt

This lovely, delicate quilt is actually very simple to construct. Hand-appliqué makes it extra special, and you may make it any size you wish by referring to the cutting charts for twin through king sizes. Finished quilt sizes: Twin, 62″ × 91″. Full, 77″ × 105″. Queen, 80″ × 108″. King, 91″ × 119″. Finished block size: 13½″ × 13½″, including seam allowances.

Closeup of block, showing details.

Materials Required

- *All purpose threads to match fabrics*
- *18-inch pillow form*

Yards of Fabric Needed, by Quilt Size

Fabric	Twin	Full or Queen	King
Dark green print	3	3½	3½
Light green print	1½	2	2½
Pink print	3	3½	3½
Lavender print	1½	2	2½
Floral print	3	4	4½
Natural (lt. tan) solid	1½	2	2½
Batting	64″ × 95″	85″ × 112″	98″ × 120″
Backing fabric	64″ × 95″	85″ × 112″	98″ × 120″
Extra-wide double-fold quilt binding	9	11	14

Directions

All seam allowances are ¼-inch and are included in all given measurements. The full-size appliqué pieces also include the ¼-inch seam allowances, as they are planned for hand appliqué. [*Note:* If you decide to use machine appliqué, remove the ¼-inch seam allowances from the appliqué pieces *only*, and proceed as described in the introductory section on machine appliqué (p. 18).]

Quilt Instructions

Each quilt is made up of blocks, which are separated by sashing and surrounded by three borders. Each block has a natural-color center pieced to two light-green and two dark-green triangles. A spinning flower is appliquéd over the pieced block (Figure 1-1).

1. Referring to Table 1, cut the required number of squares for the size of quilt you will be making.
2. Fold each natural block in quarters on the diagonal and press it to mark the center of the block (Figure 1-2). Referring to Figure 1-3, cut each light-green square in half on the diagonal to form two triangles. You will have 30 light-green triangles for the twin-size quilt, 48 for the full or queen-size, and 70 for the king-size. Repeat this with the dark-green squares to make an equal number of triangles (30, 48, or 70). You will now have 2 triangles of light green and two of dark green for each block (Figure 1-3).

Table 1. Number and Size of Squares to Cut to Make the Blocks, by Quilt Size

	Twin	Full or Queen	King
Natural block centers, 9½″ × 9½″	15	24	35
Light green squares, 7″ × 7″	15	24	35
Dark green squares, 7″ × 7″	15	24	35

1–1. Diagram of a block. Each block will be 13½″ × 13½″, including seam allowances.

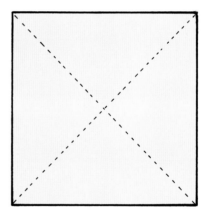

1–2. Fold each natural-colored square on the diagonals and press to mark the centers.

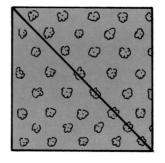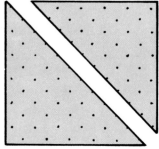

1–3. Cut each light-green and dark-green square into two triangles along one diagonal.

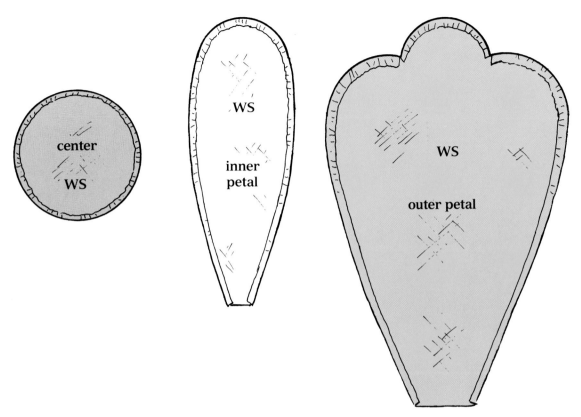

1–4. *Turn seam allowances to the wrong sides of the petal and center appliqués and baste the seam allowances in place.*

3. Trace out the appliqué patterns (p. 35, 36) onto cardboard or plastic for making templates and cut them out. Cut the required number of appliqué pieces from fabric for the size of quilt you are making (see Table 2).

Table 2. Number of Appliqué Pieces to Cut, by Quilt Size

Piece	Twin	Full or Queen	King
Lavender flower center	15	24	35
Pink outer petal	60	96	140
Floral print inner petal	60	96	140

4. Referring to the section on appliqué in the Techniques chapter at the beginning of the book, turn the seam allowances of each large and small petal to the wrong side of the petal fabric, and hand-baste it in place with large running stitches, leaving the narrow bottom edge (without the seam allowance) unturned. Press the petals. Turn under the raw edges of the lavender flower centers and baste them as well (Figure 1-4).

5. Appliqué one inner petal, centered, to each outer petal by hand, using natural-colored thread, with the raw edges at the narrow ends of both petals aligned. Afterwards, remove the basting thread from the inner petals only and press the petals (Figure 1-5).

6. With ¼" seam allowances, stitch two light-green triangles to opposite sides of each natural block (Figure 1-6). Press the seam allowances towards the green fabric. Stitch two dark-green triangles to the two remaining sides of each natural block and press them.

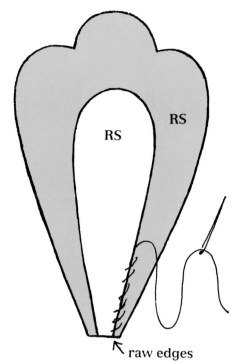

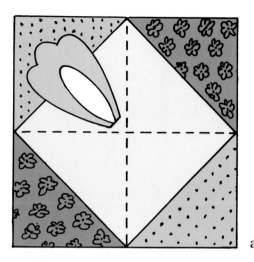

1–5. *Center the inner petal on the outer petal with raw edges aligned, and hand-appliqué the inner one to the outer one.*

1–7. a: *Appliquéing a petal unit in place, ½-inch away from the natural-colored square's center.* **b:** *The finished block with all 4 petal units in place, and a center circle appliquéd over them.*

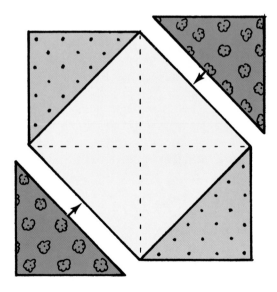

1–6. *Stitch two light-green rectangles to opposite sides of a natural-colored square; then stitch two dark-green triangles to the remaining sides.*

7. Appliqué one completed petal to each of the 4 quarters of each block by hand, using matching thread. When you place the petals on the blocks, the raw-edged, narrow end of each petal unit should be ½-inch from the center of each natural square (Figure 1-7a). It's alright if the inner ends of the petals touch or overlap slightly. Appliqué one lavender flower center to the center of each block with lavender thread, covering the raw edges of the petals with the piece (Figure 1-7b).

8. Repeat Step 7 until all of the blocks have been appliquéd.

1-8. *Twin-size quilt: stitch a row with 3 blocks and 4 vertical sashing strips, as shown here. Repeat to total 5 rows.*

1–9. *Full or queen-size quilt: stitch a row with 4 blocks and 5 vertical sashing strips, as shown here. Repeat to total 6 rows.*

1–10. *King-size quilt: stitch a row with 5 blocks and 6 vertical sashing strips, as shown here. Repeat to total 7 rows.*

9. The finished block size is 13½″ × 13½″. Cut the vertical and horizontal sashing strips for the quilt from lavender fabric, referring to Table 3 to see how many and what size. Go to step 10T for twin-sized quilt, 10F or Q for the full or queen-sized quilt, and to 10K for the king-size quilt instructions.

10T. For the twin-size quilt, make a row of 3 blocks alternating with 4 vertical sashing strips (each 1½″ × 13½″), as shown in Figure 1–8. Make 4 more rows the same way, for a total of 5 rows.

10F or Q. For the full- or queen-size quilt, make a row of 4 blocks, alternating with 5 vertical sashing strips (each 1½″ × 13½″) for each row, as shown in Figure 1-9. Make 5 more rows in the same way, for a total of 6 rows.

10K. For the king-size quilt, make a row of 5 blocks alternating with 6 vertical sashing strips (each 1½″ × 13½″), as shown in Figure 1-10. Make 6 more rows the same way, for a total of 7 rows.

11. To assemble the quilt center, join the block rows, made in step 10, alternating with the horizontal sashing strips, cut earlier. An assembly diagram of the twin-size quilt is shown in Figure 1-11. The full- and queen-sized quilts are assembled in the same manner but have 6 rows of 4 blocks each (see Figure 1-13 for reference). The king-sized quilt has 7 rows of 5 blocks each but is assembled in the same way (see Figure 1-14 for reference). Remember to press each seam after stitching.

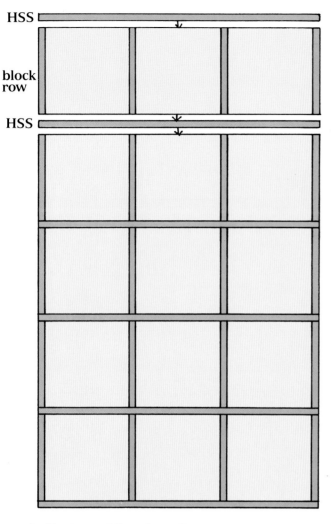

HSS

block row

HSS

1–11. *Assembling the quilt center for the twin-size quilt. The assembled rows of blocks are alternated with the horizontal sashing strips (HSS). The same method is used for all quilt sizes. See construction diagrams for the layout of full-, queen- and king-size quilts.*

Table 3. Cutting Guide for Lavender Sashing Strips, by Quilt Size

Sashing	Number to cut	Size
Twin-Size Quilt		
Vertical	20	1½″ × 13½″
Horizontal	6	1½″ × 43½″
Full- or Queen-Size Quilt		
Vertical	30	1½″ × 13½″
Horizontal	7	1½″ × 57½″
King-Size Quilt		
Vertical	42	1½″ × 13½″
Horizontal	8	1½″ × 71½″

12. Referring to the border cutting chart (Table 4), cut the border strips for the quilt.

13. Stitch the borders to the quilt center, following the construction diagram for each size. Attach the top and bottom border strip for each border first; then the side ones (Figure 1-12). Press the seams after each addition; always press the seam allowances towards the darker fabrics. See the full- and queen-

Table 4. Cutting Chart for Borders

Quilt Size	Inner Border (Pink Print) No.	Inner Border (Pink Print) Size	Central Border (Dark Green) No.	Central Border (Dark Green) Size	Outer Border (Floral Print) No.	Outer Border (Floral Print) Size
Twin	2	1½″ × 71½″	2	2½″ × 73½″	2	7½″ × 77½″
	2	1½″ × 45½″	2	2½″ × 49½″	2	7½″ × 63½″
Full	2	1½″ × 85½″	2	2½″ × 87½″	2	7½″ × 91½″
	2	1½″ × 59½″	2	2½″ × 63½″	2	7½″ × 77½″
Queen	2	2½″ × 85½″	2	3½″ × 89½″	2	7″ × 95½″
	2	2½″ × 61½″	2	3½″ × 67½″	2	7″ × 80″
King	2	1½″ × 99½″	2	2½″ × 101½″	2	7½″ × 105½″
	2	1½″ × 73½″	2	2½″ × 77½″	2	7½″ × 91½″

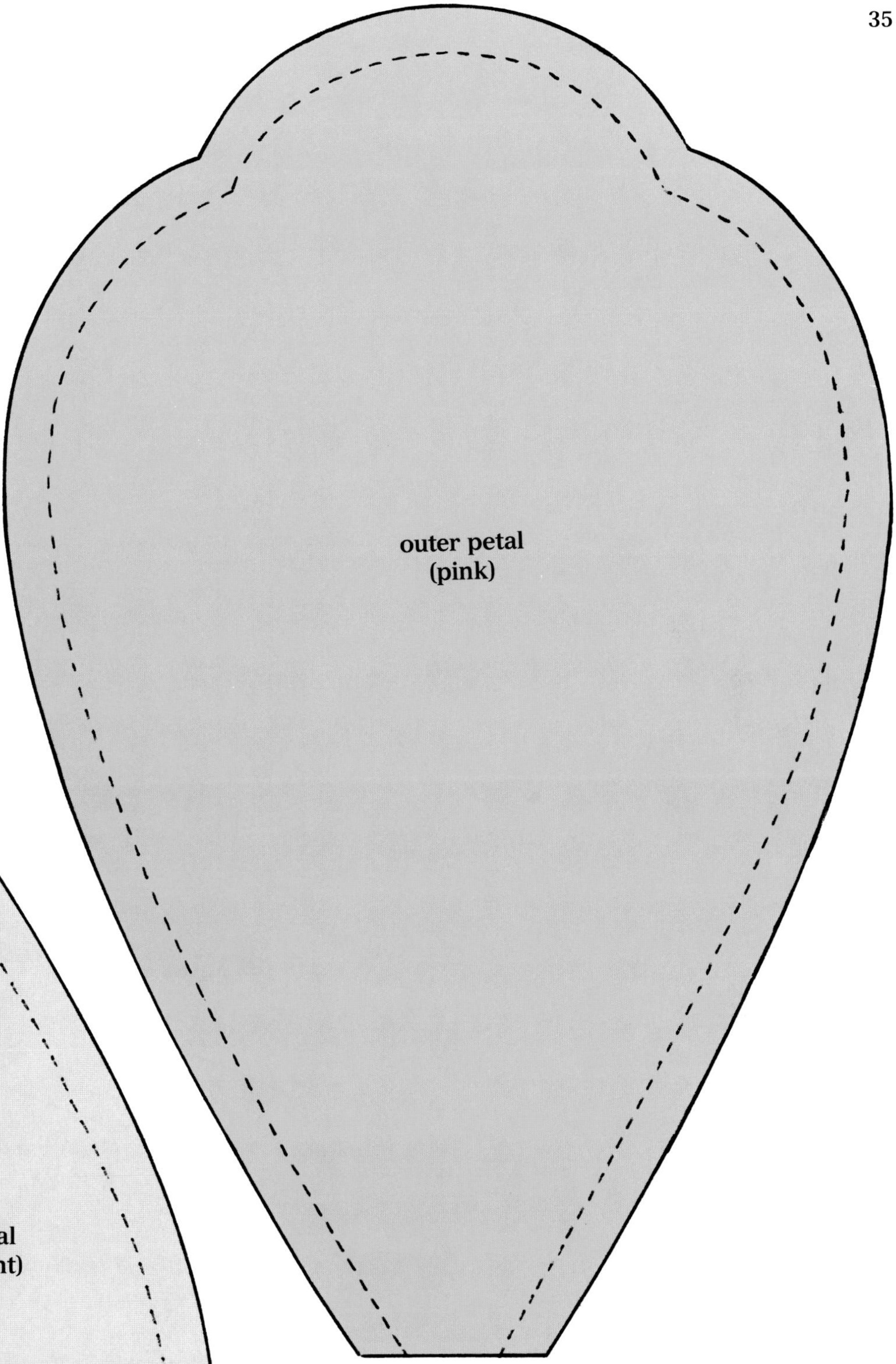

outer petal
(pink)

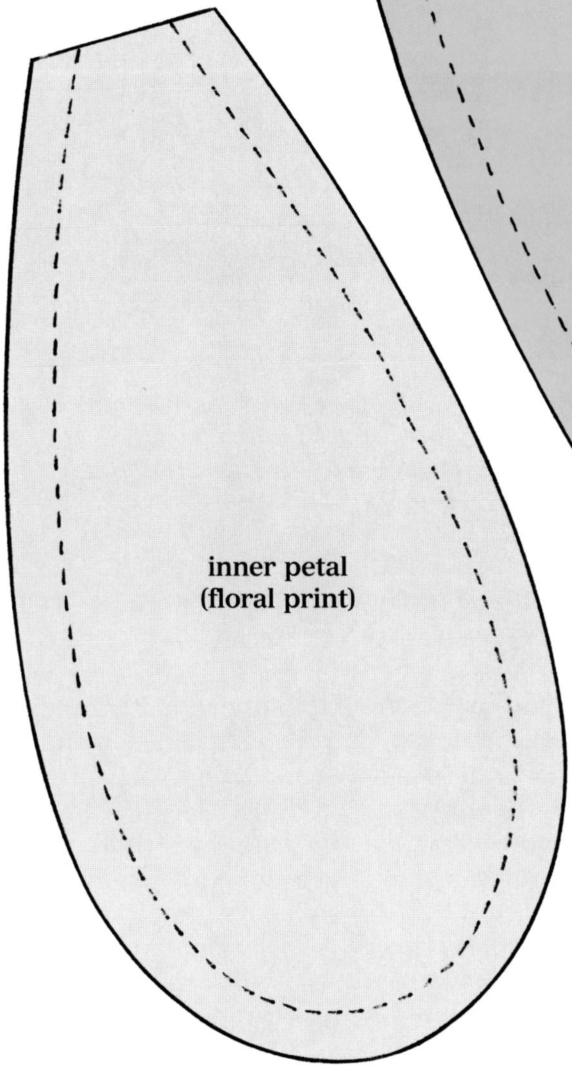

inner petal
(floral print)

Full-size appliqué patterns for petals of the Spinning Flowers Quilt. Dashed line is seamline; solid line is cutting line.

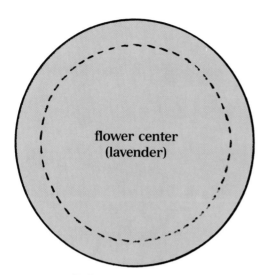

Full-size appliqué pattern
for flower center.

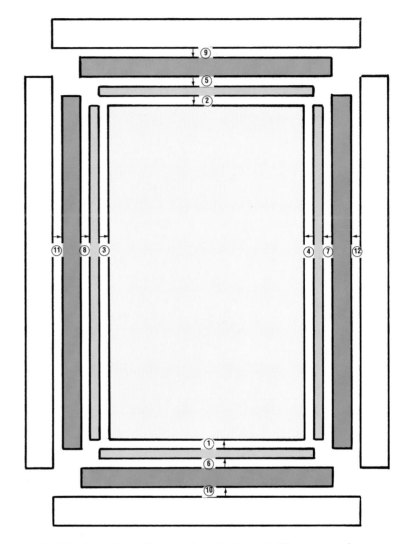

1–12. Attaching the borders (all sizes). The top and bottom of each border are attached first; then the side strips are added. Circled numbers indicate order of piecing. IB, inner border; CB, central border; OB, outer border.

sized construction diagram (Figure 1-13) or the king-size construction diagram (Figure 1-14) for reference. To assemble the layers for basting, lay the backing fabric face-down on a clean floor. Tape the backing fabric to the floor at the corners and midway along each side to keep it from shifting. Center the batting on the backing, allowing the batting to expand on its own after you unfold it for about ½-hour before you proceed. Center the quilt top face-up over the batting, taping it to the floor as you did for the backing fabric. Pin-baste or hand-baste the quilt through all 3 layers, starting at the center of the quilt and working outwards. (See basting instructions in the "Techniques" chapter.)

15. Hand- or machine-quilt the quilt as you desire, or quilt along all seam lines, around each appliqué piece, and again ¼-inch from the first lines of quilting. See the "Techniques" chapter for quilting instructions.

16. Baste all around the outer edge close to the raw edges of the quilt top; then trim away any excess batting and backing fabric. Bind the quilt with the bias binding to complete it. (See binding instructions in the "Techniques" chapter.)

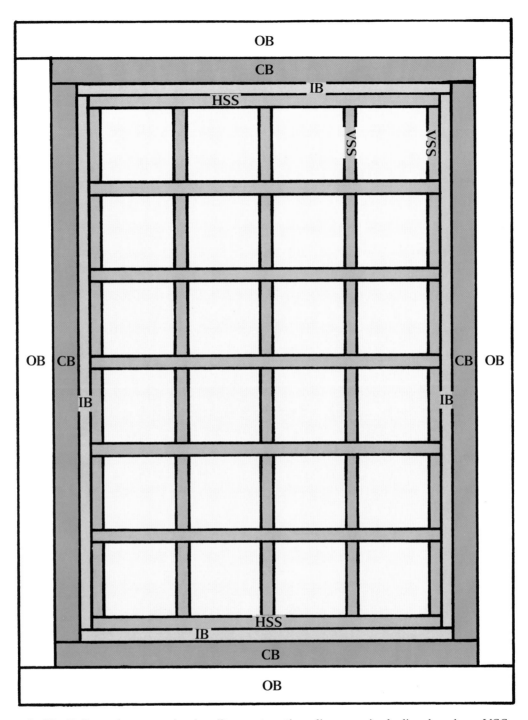

1–13. Full- and queen-sized quilt construction diagram, including borders. VSS, vertical sashing strip; HSS, horizontal sashing strip; IB, inner border strip; CB, central border strip; OB, outer border strip.

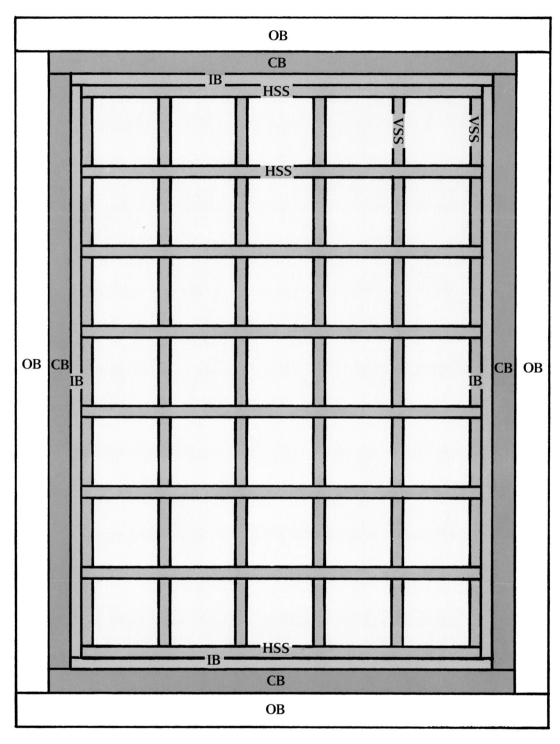

1–14. *King-size quilt construction diagram, including borders. VSS, vertical sashing strip; HSS, horizontal sashing strip; IB, inner border strip; CB, central border strip; OB, outer border strip.*

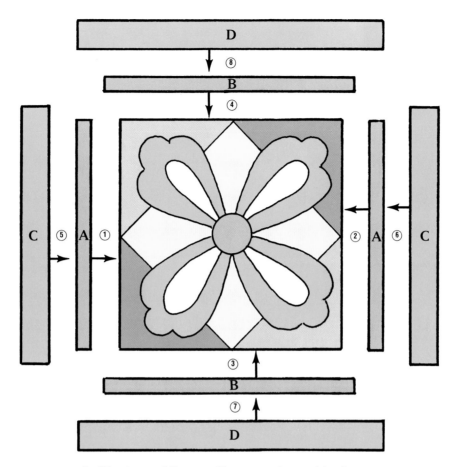

1–15. *Assembling a pillow top. Assemble the inner (lavender) borders and then the outer (pink print) borders. Circled numbers indicate the order of piecing.*

Pillow Instructions

1. To make a matching 18-inch pillow from the scrap yardage, cut and appliqué one block as you did for the quilt (see quilt instructions steps 1 through 7). It should be 13½″ × 13½″ when you complete it.

2. Then, from the lavender fabric, cut 2 A strips, 1½″ × 13½″ each, and stitch one strip to two opposite sides of the appliquéd block (Figure 1-15). Cut two B strips 1½″ × 15½″ each from the lavender fabric and stitch them to the remaining 2 sides of the unit. Press.

3. From the pink print fabric cut 2 C strips, 2″ × 15½″ each, and 2 D strips, 2″ × 18½″ each, for outer borders; attach them to the unit

made in Step 2, joining the C strips to the sides first (see Figure 1-15). Press the unit.

4. To make the ruffle, cut 4 strips of any fabric you choose, 6½″ × 40″ each, and stitch them together on their short ends to form a long strip (Figure 1-16a). Join the outer short ends to make a circular band of cloth. Press the seam allowances open. Fold the band in half along its length with wrong sides of fabric together, so the raw edges of both sides of the band meet and the short seams are aligned. Press. Run basting stitches through both thicknesses of the band at the raw edges and gather it to fit the pillow's perimeter. Place the ruffle on the pillow front, aligning the raw

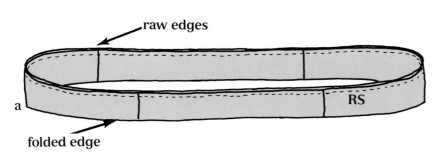

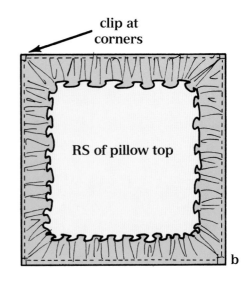

1–16. *Making and attaching the pillow ruffle.* **a:** *Seam strips together to make a band, fold lengthwise and gather.* **b:** *Attach ruffle to pillow top, distributing the ruffle evenly.*

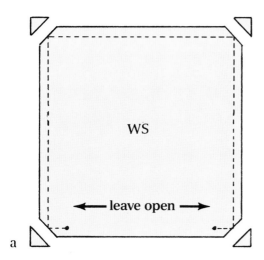

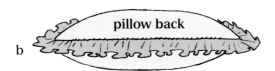

1–17. **a:** *Trim the seam allowance at the corners close to, but not through, the stitching to reduce bulk.* **b:** *After the pillow form is inserted in the cover, stitch the opening closed by hand.*

edges of the ruffle with the raw edges of the pillow front, and clipping into the ¼-inch seam allowance of the ruffle at the corners. Distribute the ruffles evenly and baste the ruffle to the pillow top ¼-inch from the edges (Figure 1-16b).

5. Cut a piece of fabric 18½″ × 18½″ from the remaining yardage to make the pillow backing. Stitch the pillow front to the backing along 3 sides, with right sides of fabric together. Clip the corners of the seam allowances (Figure 1-17a) and turn the pillow cover right-side out through the opening. Insert an 18″ × 18″ pillow form and hand-stitch the opening closed (Figure 1-17b).

Heart Pillow with Silk Flowers

For a breath of spring at any time of year, make this pillow in your favorite colors to brighten up a couch or chair, or as a present for someone special. Finished size of pillow: Approximately 16″ × 14″, excluding ruffle.

Materials Required

- *18″ × 18″ square natural-colored solid fabric*
- *18″ × 18″ square backing fabric of your choice*
- *18″ × 18″ square of fleece or quilt batting*
- *1 yard natural-colored floral print fabric for ruffle*
- *Assorted silk roses*
- *Bits of ¼″-wide satin ribbon*
- *Polyester fiberfill for stuffing*
- *3 yards of pink piping*

Directions

The seam allowances for this project are ¼-inch.

1. Enlarge the heart pattern from page 43, referring to the section on "Enlarging a Grid Pattern" in the Basic Techniques chapter for guidance, and cut it out of folded paper or cardboard.

2. Using the enlarged heart pattern, cut the heart shape from the natural-colored solid fabric. Baste the heart you just cut to the fleece square and trim away the excess fleece. Cut another heart from the backing fabric as well.

3. Baste the piping all around the edge of the right side of the pillow front; the raw edges of the piping should be aligned with the raw edge of the pillow front. Overlap the raw edges of the fabric of the piping where the ends meet; trim the inner cord to the correct length so the cord ends butt; and slipstitch the fabric ends of the piping together by hand so one covers the other and the raw edges are turned under.

4. To make the ruffle, cut 3 strips, 11″ × 44″ each, from the floral print fabric. Stitch the 3 strips together along their short ends to make one long strip. Fold the strip in half along its length, with the right sides together, so its folded size is 5½″ × 130″. Stitch across the short ends (Figure 2-1a). Trim off the corners of the seam allowances close to, but not through, the stitching line. Turn the strip right-side out and press. Gather it along the double raw edges (Figure 2-1b) until it fits around the pillow. (Position the center of the ruffle at the heart's point.)

5. Baste the ruffle to the pillow front over the piping, starting and finishing at the top of the heart and distributing the ruffles evenly (Figure 2-2).

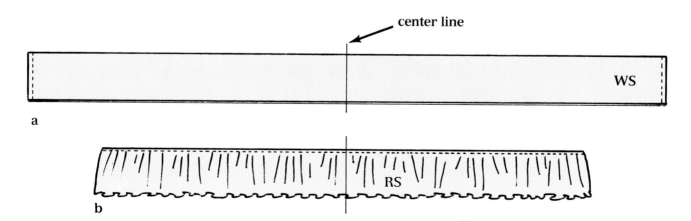

*2–1. The ruffle. **a:** The joined strip is folded right-side in along its long edge and its center is marked. Stitch along its short ends. Turn it right side out. **b:** Gather the strip along its double raw edge.*

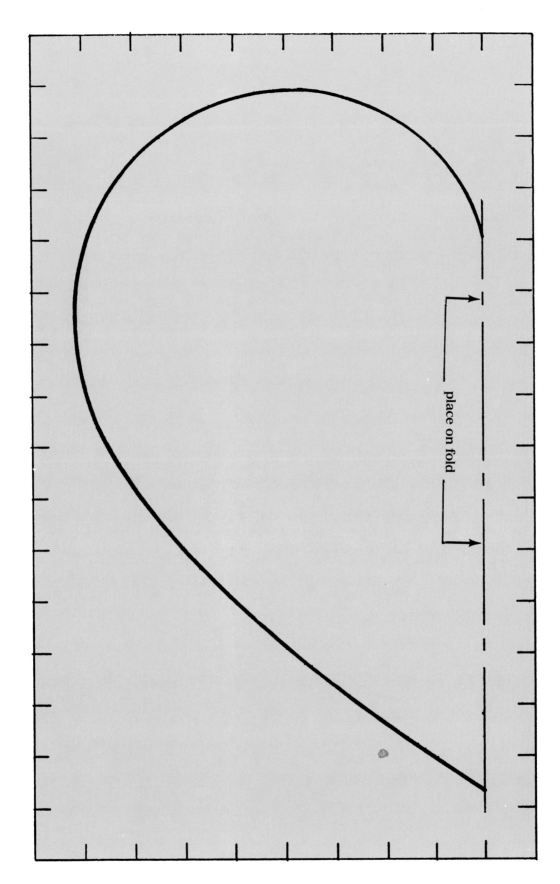

place on fold

Half of the reduced heart pattern. One box = 1″ × 1″. Enlarge the pattern and cut one template on folded paper or plastic.

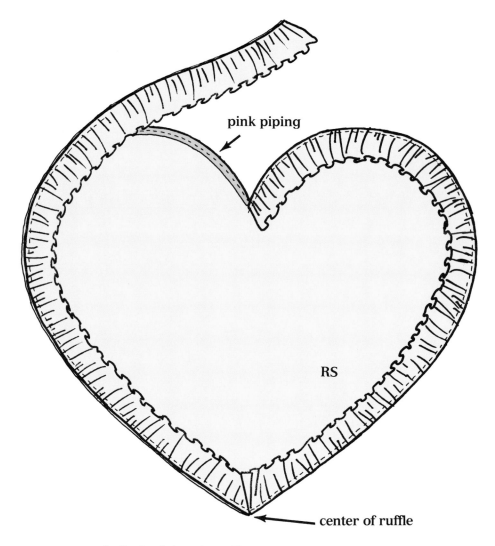

2–2. Applying the ruffle to the pillow front. Place the center of the ruffle at the point of the heart.

6. Pin and then stitch the pillow front to the pillow back, with right sides together. Leave a 4″ opening along one side for turning the pillow cover right-side out. Clip the curves of the seam allowance, turn the pillow cover right-side out, and press it. Stuff it firmly with fiberfill; then hand-stitch the turning opening closed.

7. Glue or baste several silk flowers to the top area of the heart at the "V" (see photo). Glue or baste bits of ribbon to the pillow so that they begin near the flowers; twist the ribbons slightly and then secure the ends to the pillow front.

Appliquéd Bath Ensemble

You can make this set quickly and easily in the colors shown here—or customize them by matching the colors in your own bathroom. They would make a lovely bridal or housewarming gift to a special friend.

The materials listed below are sufficient for 4 towels, 1 hanger cover, and 1 bathroom tissue cover. The tissue cover stands 4″ tall and fits a standard roll of toilet tissue.

Materials Required

Towels

- *2 white bath towels and 2 white hand towels*
- *¼ yard of light pink print fabric*
- *¼ yard of dark pink solid fabric*
- *Scraps of yellow fabric*
- *Scraps of green fabric*
- *½ yard fusible transfer webbing*
- *Threads to match the fabrics*
- *1½ yards 1″-wide flat white lace*
- *Stabilizer (see the Necessary Supplies chapter)*

Additional Materials to Make Hanger Covers and Bathroom Tissue Cover

- *⅔ yard white fabric (for hanger cover)*
- *⅔ yard fleece or batting*
- *10″ length of ¼″-wide pink satin ribbon*
- *15″ of ½″-wide flat lace that coordinates with the lace for the towels*
- *Wooden hangers with removable metal hanging loops*
- *¾ yard white fabric (for tissue cover)*

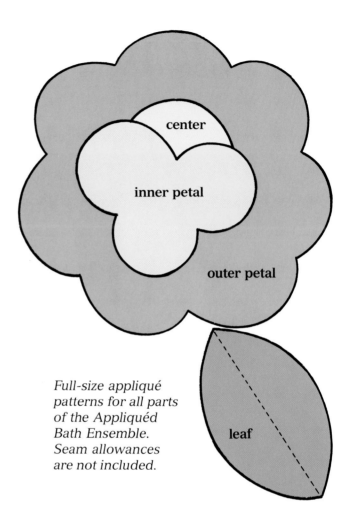

Full-size appliqué patterns for all parts of the Appliquéd Bath Ensemble. Seam allowances are not included.

Directions

The seam allowances used in the hanger cover and tissue cover are ¼″. The bath towels do not require seam allowances.

Towels

1. Trace out onto template cardboard or plastic the appliqué patterns of the outer petal, the inner petal, the flower center, and the leaf from the appliqué pattern above. Cut out each pattern, and label its top side.

2. For *each* towel, trace onto the paper side of fusible webbing the reversed patterns of: 3 outer petals, 3 inner petals, 3 flower centers, and the correct number of leaves (8 for bath towels, 4 for hand towels). Cut them all out of the webbing.

Closeup of towel appliqué.

3. For each towel, fuse two webbing outer petals onto the back of light pink fabric and one onto the back of dark pink fabric (see color photo). Or reverse this order and fuse two outer petals onto the back of dark pink fabric and one onto light pink fabric (see color photo, right). Fuse the webbing inner petals onto the tint of pink fabric that contrasts with the outer petals (see photo). Fuse the webbing flower centers to the back of the yellow fabric (you need a total of 12 centers for 4 towels). Fuse the webbing leaves onto the back of the green fabric.

4. Cut out all the shapes fused in Step 3; they will be appliquéd on.

5. Referring to Figure 3-1, position the appliqués, face-up, on the towels, and fuse them in place. (Note the position of the towel bands in Figure 3-1.) See the Basic Techniques chapter section on machine appliqué for reference. Back the appliqué areas with stabilizer.

6. Machine-appliqué the pieces in place, using shades of thread that match each fabric and a medium-width satin stitch. Appliqué in the order of outer petals, flower centers, inner petals, leaves. When you stitch the leaves, satin-stitch down the center of the leaves from point to point on each to make the veins of the leaves. Remove the stabilizer after you have appliquéd all the pieces in place.

7. Measure across the bottom edge of each towel and add 1″ to your measurement to get the length of lace required to trim the bottom of the towel. Cut the length of lace required and fold in ½″ on each short side of the lace towards the wrong side of the lace. Stitch the lace to the *back* side of the towel so it overlaps the bottom towel edge ¼″, with the turned-in ends of the lace facing away from the front of the towel. The lace should hang down ¾″ beyond the bottom edge of the towel. Repeat this for all of the towels.

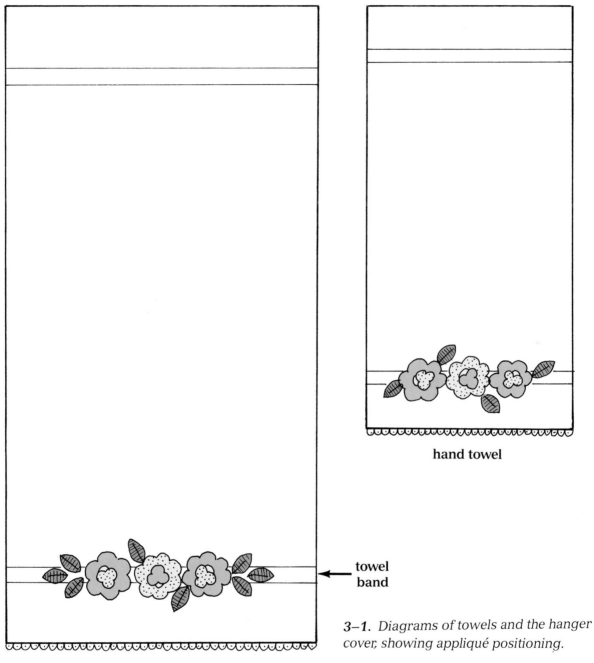

towel
band

3–1. *Diagrams of towels and the hanger cover, showing appliqué positioning.*

bath towel

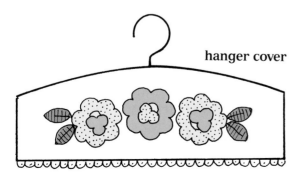

hanger cover

Hanger Cover

1. To make the hanger cover, cut a 6″ × 18″ strip of white fabric. Lay the hanger on the strip with the top of the wooden portion of the hanger ½″ from the top long edge of the strip and the hanger centered on the 18″ width of the fabric. Trace along the curve of the wooden portion of the hanger to mark the curve on the fabric (see Figure 3-2a). Mark the fabric where

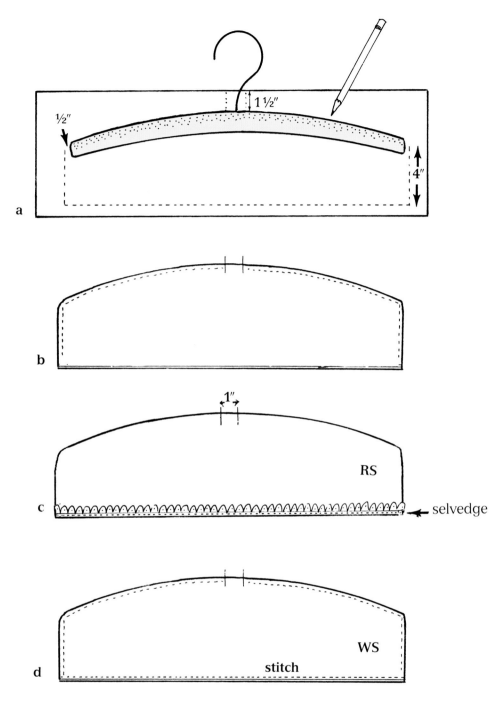

3–2. **a:** *Place the hanger on the fabric and mark the cover shape (dashed line). Trace along the top edge of the hanger to mark the curve also.* **b:** *The fleeced hanger outer cover, showing the opening at the top for the hanger. Stitch the two pieces together as shown (dashed line).* **c:** *Baste lace around the bottom edge of the outer cover on the right side, with the selvedge facing out, as shown.* **d:** *Turn the outer cover right-side out. Slip the lining over it, wrong-side out; align the raw edges. Stitch the lining and outer cover together along the entire bottom edge. Turn the unit right-side out through the hanger opening.*

the wire hanger curve extends from the wooden portion of the hanger, and make a mark ½″ from either side of the hanger mark (Figure 3-2a). Make another mark ½″ from each outer end of the wooden arms of the hanger. Make a 4″ vertical line down from the side of the hanger at the mark you just made below each hanger arm. Draw a horizontal line to connect the vertical lines (Figure 3-2a). Cut out the resulting hanger cover shape from the fabric (Figure 3-2b).

Draw a horizontal line to connect the vertical lines (Figure 3-2a). Cut out the resulting hanger cover shape from the fabric (Figure 3-2b).

2. Using the shape cut in Step 1 as a pattern, cut out 3 more white fabric pieces of the same shape, for a total of 4 white fabric shapes. Also cut 2 of the same shape from fleece.

3. Trace 3 sets of flower appliqués from the reversed patterns and 4 leaves onto the paper side of fusible webbing and cut the shapes out of the webbing. Fuse the webbing shapes to the backs of the correct fabrics (see color photo for reference) and cut them out.

4. Using Figure 3-1 for reference, fuse the flowers and leaves to the front of one piece of the white fabric cut in Step 2 for the hanger cover. Machine appliqué the flowers and leaves in place (see Step 6 of the Towel instructions for reference) to make the hanger front.

5. Baste one fleece shape (cut in Step 2) to the wrong side of the hanger front that you just appliquéd; baste the second fleece shape to the wrong side of another hanger cover shape (cut in Step 2). Stitch the two fleeced shapes together, with right sides of fabric facing and the fleece out, along the side seams and the top seam (see Figure 3-2b), leaving the top seam unstitched between at the 1″-wide center, which will be the hanger wire opening. Clip the

curves in the hanger cover seam allowances and turn the cover right-side out. Press it.

6. Baste lace around the bottom edge of hanger cover with the selvedge edge of the lace even with the raw edge of the hanger cover and the decorative ends of the lace facing the curved edge of the hanger cover (Figure 3-2c). This completes the outer cover unit.

7. Stitch the two remaining white hanger cover shapes (cut in Step 2) together along their side and top edges, leaving a 1″-wide hanger wire opening unstitched along the top edge, as you did for the outer cover unit, to make the hanger lining.

8. Place the fleeced hanger cover section and the lining together, with right sides facing, and stitch along the straight (bottom) edge (Figure 3-2d). Be sure not to catch the free (decorative) length of the lace.

9. Turn the hanger cover right-side out through the opening made for the wire. Push the lining into the hanger cover and stitch along the bottom edge of the cover, near the lace, to prevent the layers from shifting.

10. Unscrew or otherwise remove the hanger wire from the wooden portion. Insert the wooden portion of the hanger in the cover, placing it against the top curved edge. Insert the hanger wire through the hole in the cover and screw it into the hanger.

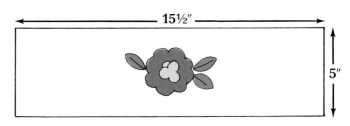

3–3. The white fabric strip for the bathroom tissue cover, showing the positioning of the appliqué.

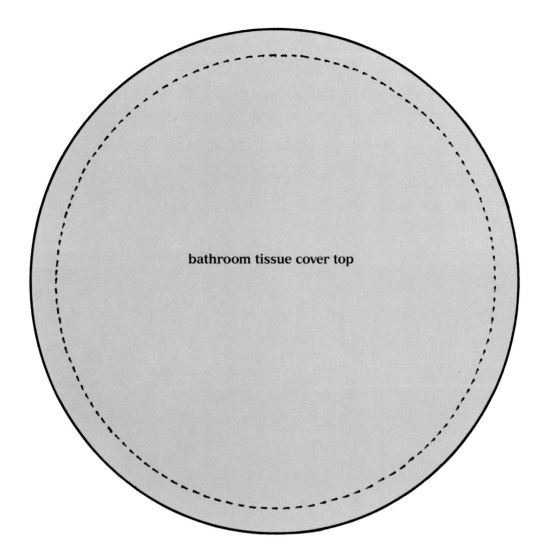

bathroom tissue cover top

Pattern for top of bathroom tissue cover. The dashed line is the sewing line; the solid line is the cutting line.

Bathroom Tissue Cover

1. From white fabric, cut two 5″ × 15½″ strips and 2 top circles, using the pattern provided above. Cut one 5″ × 15½″ piece of fleece and one circular top of fleece also.

2. From the appliqué pattern (p. 46), trace one reversed flower and 3 leaves onto the paper side of fusible webbing and cut them out of the webbing. Cut, fuse, and appliqué one flower to the center of one white strip (cut in Step 1), as shown in Figure 3-3. See the appliqué instructions in steps 1–6 of the Towel instructions for guidance.

3. Baste the fleece strip cut in Step 1 to the wrong side of the appliquéd strip. Baste the fleece top circle cut in Step 1 to the wrong side of one white fabric top circle.

4. Fold the appliquéd strip together so its short ends align, with the right sides of appliquéd fabric facing each other, and stitch it together on its short sides to make a tube. Press the seam allowance open. Repeat this with the plain fabric strip cut in Step 1.

5. Pin and baste the fleece top to the fleeced tube, with right sides together and ¼″ seam

allowances (Figure 3-4). Stitch the top to the tube. This makes the outer cover.

6. Pin, baste, and stitch the second white fabric top circle to the second white fabric tube in the same way as you did for the fleeced pieces in Step 5. This makes the lining unit.

7. Turn the fleeced outer cover right-side out. Place the outer cover and lining unit together, with right sides facing, and stitch them together along the open bottom edge, leaving a 2″ turning opening along the edge at the back of the cover. Then turn the unit right-side out through the opening, and stitch the opening closed by hand.

8. Baste the ½″-wide lace to the bottom edge of the outside of the tissue cover (Figure 3-5).

9. Tie the 10″ piece of ribbon into a bow and tack it to the top center of the tissue cover to complete it.

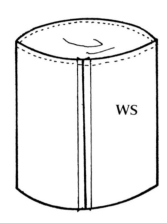

3–4. The wrong side of the bathroom tissue cover (outer layer), showing stitching lines joining the top and the strip.

3–5. The outside of the tissue cover, showing the lace at the bottom.

Watermelon Table Runner

This runner makes a delightful addition to your summer table, and works up very quickly. The finished size of the runner is 18″ × 42″. The finished size of a napkin is 18″ × 18″.

Materials Required

- *18½" × 42½" rectangle of white fabric*

- *18½" × 42½" rectangle of fabric of choice for backing*

- *¼ yard green fabric*

- *½ yard pink fabric*

- *19" square of fabric of choice for each napkin*

- *¾ yard fusible transfer webbing*

- *All-purpose threads to match fabrics, plus black*

- *Black 6-strand cotton embroidery floss*

- *4 yards of green double-fold bias binding (¼"-wide when finished, 1"-wide when opened out)*

- *4 yards of black soutache or middy braid (you may also substitute ⅛"-wide satin ribbon if the braids are not available)*

- *18½" × 42½" rectangle of fleece*

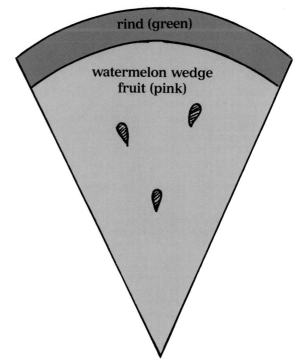

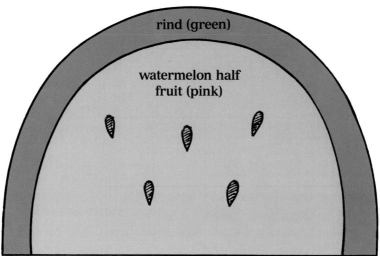

Full-size appliqué patterns for the watermelon half and wedge. (No seam allowances are included.)

Directions

All markings on fabric should be done in washable pen or pencil.

1. From the appliqué patterns on page 54, trace 4 watermelon halves (both fruit and rind) onto the paper side of fusible webbing; trace 24 each of the fruit and rind of the watermelon wedges onto the webbing also. Cut all the pieces out of the webbing. Fuse the webbing fruit pieces to the back of the pink fabric and the webbing rinds to the back of the green fabric. Cut the fused shapes out of the fabrics. Transfer the embroidery markings for the seeds to each pink shape from the patterns.

2. Referring to Figure 4-1, mark a line 1½″ in from each edge on the 18½″ × 42½″ white fabric rectangle. This is the placement line for the black braid, which will be stitched in place later.

3. Pin or baste one pink fabric watermelon fruit half at each corner of the white rectangle, as shown in the photo and Figure 4-1. Place the green half-circle fabric rind just under the rounded edge of the pink fabric fruit half-circle . The rind should be exactly 1″ in from the marked braid lines (see Figure 4-1).

4. Pin or baste two pink watermelon fruit wedges, with rinds underneath, between each watermelon half on the *short* ends of the runner (see photo and Figure 4-1). Pin and baste 10 fruit wedges, with rinds underneath, between the watermelon halves at the runner corners, along each *long* side of the runner. The outside edge of the rinds should be 1″ from the marked braid line; the wedges should be evenly spaced along each side. Fuse all the pieces in place.

5. Machine-appliqué the pieces in place with threads that match the fabrics.

6. Satin-stitch the watermelon seeds by hand, using 2 strands of the 6-strand embroidery floss in your embroidery needle. (A closeup of the satin stitch is shown in Figure 4-2.)

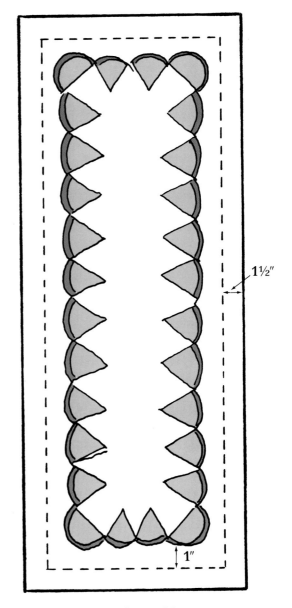

4–1. *Diagram of the table runner, showing the line for braid attachment, 1½″ in from the perimeter, and the positioning of watermelon appliqués, 1″ in from the braid line.*

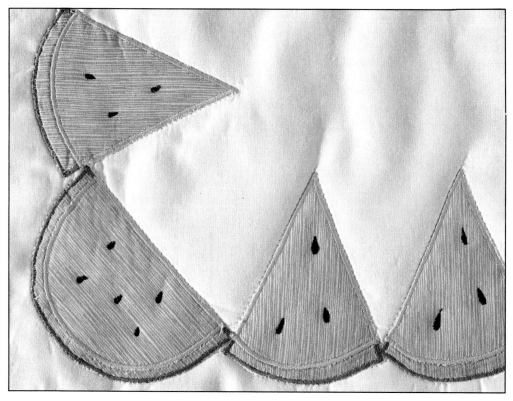

Closeup of runner corner, showing appliqué details

7. Baste the fleece rectangle to the wrong side of the appliquéd runner. Place the backing rectangle face-down on your work surface and center the fleeced, appliquéd runner top face-up over the backing piece; pin them together. Baste around the outside to join both rectangles, close to the raw edges. Pin the bias binding to the front of the runner with right sides of the binding fabric facing the right side of the runner and raw edges aligned. Stitch around the outside ¼″ in from the edge. Turn the unattached long edge of the bias binding to the back of the runner and secure it by hand with overcast stitching. (Refer to the Basic Techniques chapter for more information about binding.)

8. Pin or baste the braid in place on the marked lines, turning under the braid ends so no raw edges show where they meet.

With black thread, machine-stitch the braid in place through all layers. This will quilt the runner as you attach the braid.

Napkins

For each napkin, turn under ¼″ hem to the wrong side on each edge of a 19″ fabric square; turn under another ¼″ hem in the same way. Press the hems. Machine-stitch the hems to secure them.

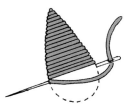

4–2. Diagram of the hand satin stitch, used for embroidering the watermelon seeds.

Apple Harvest Kitchen Set

Stitch this set up in the deep country-style colors shown here or brighten it up by using primary colors, or even pastels! The finished size of each place mat is 18″ × 12″. The finished size of a napkin is 18″ × 18″.

Materials Required for Set of Two Place Mats, Two Napkins, and a Potholder

- *Two 12½″ × 12½″ squares of light-green print fabric*
- *⅓ yard dark-green solid-color fabric*
- *¾ yard light red print fabric (includes fabric for napkins)*
- *½ yard dark red solid-color fabric*
- *Scraps of solid brown fabric for stems*
- *2 pieces of fabric for place mat backings, 14″ × 20″ each*
- *2 pieces of fleece or quilt batting for place mats, 14″ × 20″ each*
- *2 pieces of cotton batting for potholder, each 10″ × 10″*
- *2 pieces of fusible transfer webbing, each 10″ × 10″*
- *6 yards of extra-width double-fold bias binding (2″ wide when opened, ½″ wide when finished)*
- *All-purpose threads to match fabrics*
- *A small amount of loose cotton batting*

Closeup of place mat showing quilting and machine-embroidery details.

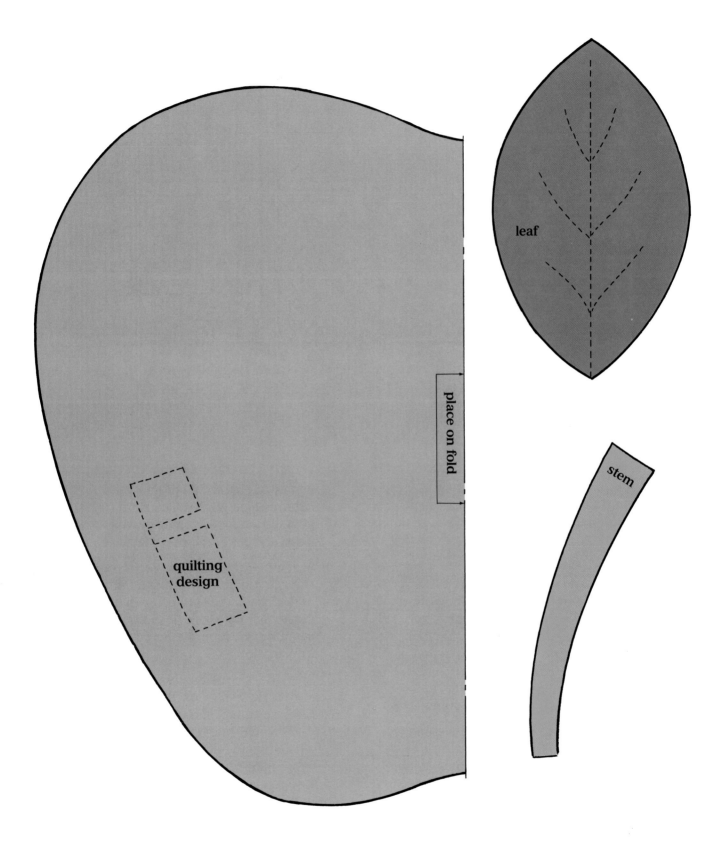

place on fold

leaf

stem

quilting design

Full-size patterns for the Apple Harvest Kitchen Set. Patterns do not include seam allowances. Dashed lines on apple and leaf are quilting optional lines. Cut apple pattern on doubled template plastic or cardboard to make a whole pattern.

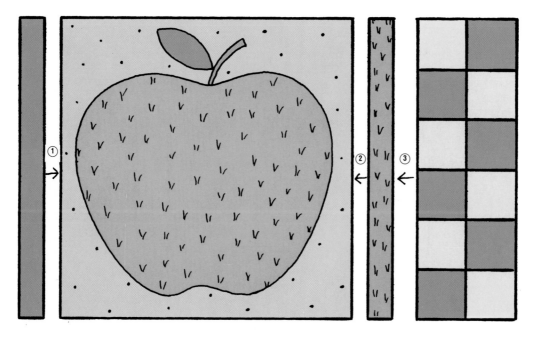

5–1. To make a place mat, join a dark green strip at left, a dark red strip at the right, and a checkered strip unit, as shown. Circled numbers indicate the order of piecing.

Directions

Seam allowances are ¼" throughout.

Place Mats

1. From the full-size patterns on page 59, trace an apple pattern, a leaf pattern, and a stem pattern onto cardboard or template plastic, cut them out, and label the right side. Reverse the patterns and trace them onto the paper side of fusible webbing; trace one leaf, one apple, and one stem onto each piece of webbing.

2. Cut the traced shapes out of the webbing. Fuse the apples to the back of the red solid-color fabric, the leaves to the back of the dark green solid-color fabric, and the stems to the backs of the dark brown scraps. Cut out the appliqué shapes from the fabrics.

3. See the Necessary Supplies chapter for information on how to use fusible transfer webbing. Fuse one set of appliqués to the center of each of the light green 12½" squares (see photo). The stem raw edge should be tucked under the apple raw edge about ¼" before fusing.

4. Machine-appliqué the pieces in place using a medium-width satin stitch and threads that match each appliqué piece. See the Basic Techniques chapter section on "Appliqué Basics" for more information.

5. From dark green solid fabric, cut two strips, 1½" × 12½" each, and from the dark red solid fabric cut two strips, 1½" × 12½" each. Stitch one dark green strip to the left-hand side of each apple block (Figure 5-1). Stitch one red strip to the right-hand side of each of the apple blocks; press the units.

6. Next we'll make the checkerboard design. From the dark green solid fabric, cut one strip 2½" × 32", and cut one 2½" × 32" strip from the light red print fabric. Place the two strips together, with right sides

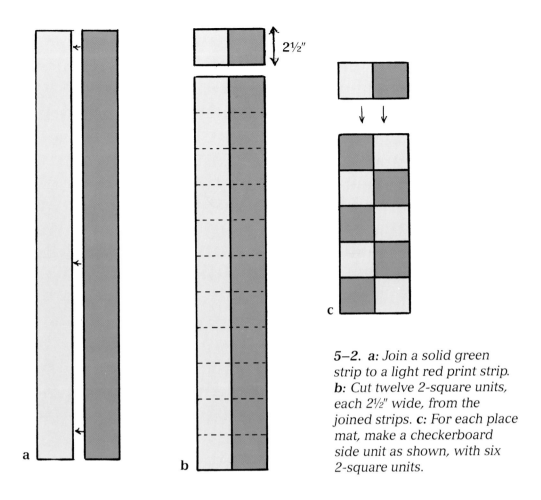

5–2. *a: Join a solid green strip to a light red print strip. b: Cut twelve 2-square units, each 2½″ wide, from the joined strips. c: For each place mat, make a checkerboard side unit as shown, with six 2-square units.*

facing, and stitch them together along one long edge, using a ¼″ seam allowance (Figure 5-2a). Press the joined strips open. Carefully mark and cut twelve 2½″-wide units of two squares each from the resulting strip (see Figure 5-2b).

7. Stitch together 6 of the 2-square units cut in Step 5, as shown in Figure 5-2c, to form a checkered side unit for the place mat. Make another checkered side unit the same way.

8. Stitch one checkered side unit to the right-hand side of each apple block unit (Figure 5-1). Press the resulting place mat top.

9. Place a 14″ × 20″ piece of place mat backing fabric face-down and center a 14″ × 20″ piece of fleece over it. Center a place mat top over the piece of fleece. Pin-baste the layers together to keep them

from shifting when you quilt. Repeat for the second place mat.

10. Quilt the place mats as you desire, by hand or machine. (See the "Quilting" section in the Basic Techniques chapter for more information.) You will notice that the patterns have quilting lines on the leaf and the apple. These are optional; use them if you wish. After quilting, baste close to the raw edges of the place mat fronts and trim away any excess fleece and backing fabric.

11. Bind the place mats with the bias binding (see the binding section in the Basic Techniques chapter).

Potholders

1. For the potholder, cut one 1″ × 6″ strip of solid brown fabric. Fold the brown strip in half lengthwise, with the right sides

together. Stitch the edges together along the long double edge only. Turn the resulting tube right-side out and press it.

2. Trace the apple shape from the pattern template made in Step 1 of the Place Mat instructions onto the wrong sides of both of the dark red 10″ squares. Cut out the apples, *adding ¼″ seam allowances around each pattern as you cut.*

3. Fold the tube made in Step 1 in half lengthwise to form a loop. Baste the loop to the top of the right side of one of the apple shapes cut in Step 2; the raw ends of the loop should extend ¼″ beyond the raw edge of the apple (see Figure 5-3).

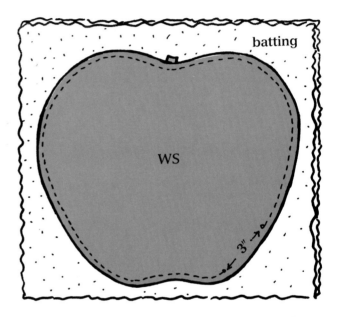

5–4. For the potholder, sew through all 4 layers to join the apple pieces to the cotton batting; leave a 3″ opening for turning the unit right-side out.

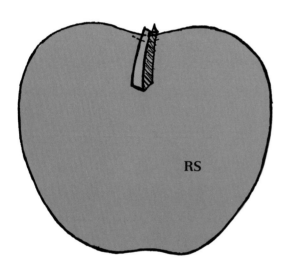

5–3. For the potholder, baste the stem loop to the top of one apple piece. Its raw edges extend ¼″ beyond the apple edge.

4. Place the two apple pieces with right sides together. Place the two squares of cotton batting together. Center the apples over the batting, pin or baste all 4 layers together, and stitch around the edges of the apples through all 4 layers, ¼″ in from the raw edges of the apples; leave a 3″ opening along one lower side for turning (see Figure 5-4). Trim away the excess batting and clip the curves of the seam allowances to ease turning (see the Basic Techniques chapter). Turn the apple right-side out and stitch the turning opening closed. Quilt the apple as shown on the pattern if you wish.

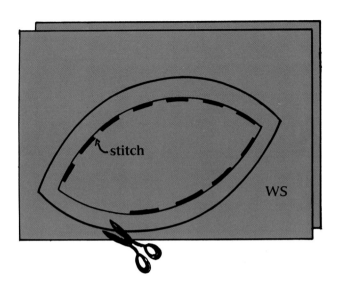

*5–5. For the potholder leaf. **a**: Stitch on the traced leaf line, keeping a 1¼" turning opening unstitched. **b**: Draw a ¼" seam allowance line around the traced and sewn leaf line; cut out the leaf unit on the outer line.*

5–6. Attach the leaf to the left of the stem.

5. For the leaf, cut two 3" × 5" pieces of dark green solid fabric. Trace the leaf onto the wrong side of one of the scraps. Place the scraps together, with right sides facing; pin the pieces together; and stitch around the traced leaf, using the marked lines as the stitching line. Leave a small opening on one side for turning (Figure 5-5). Cut the leaf out of the two-layered fabric, adding ¼" seam allowance around the leaf shape as you cut. Clip the curves of the seam allowance to ease turning, and turn the leaf right-side out. Press it. If you wish, stuff the leaf lightly with some loose cotton batting before stitching the turning opening closed. Quilt the leaf by machine or by hand if you wish (see the pattern for quilting lines).

6. Hand-stitch the leaf to the top edge of the apple, where the apple meets the stem (Figure 5-6).

Napkins

For each napkin, fold under a ¼" hem to the wrong side of a light red 19" square; fold under another ¼" to form a double hem. Stitch the hem in place and press the napkin.

Tulip Floor Cloth

Match the colors of the cloth to your own decor—or match them to a friend's for a unique gift idea!
Finished size of floor cloth: 22″ × 28″, excluding the fringe.

Materials Required

- *23″ × 29″ piece of natural-colored heavy cotton canvas or duck cloth*
- *½ yard navy blue print fabric*
- *Scraps of 5 different solid red and pink or print red and pink fabrics, totalling ⅓ yard*
- *¼ yard green print fabric*
- *½ yard fusible webbing*
- *All-purpose thread to match the fabrics*
- *4 yards of natural-colored ¼″-wide satin ribbon*
- *2 yards of 4″-wide cotton fringe*

Directions

1. Trace the flower parts and leaves onto template plastic or cardboard from the appliqué patterns on page 67, label the fronts of the patterns, and cut them out of the plastic or cardboard.

2. Trace 5 sets of the reversed flower parts (A, B, and C) onto the paper side of fusible webbing. Cut out the webbing parts. Fuse the webbing flower parts onto the wrong side of the various red and pink scraps and cut them out. Try to vary the fabrics so that each flower has 3 different fabrics.

3. Trace the leaf patterns (D, E, F, G) onto the template plastic or cardboard, label the front sides of the patterns, and cut them out of the template plastic or cardboard. Pairing the leaves randomly, trace 5 pairs of leaves from the reversed leaf patterns onto the paper side of fusible webbing, and cut them out. Fuse the webbing leaves to the wrong side of the green print fabric and cut out the leaves. Set the leaf and flower parts aside.

4. Cut the following strips from the navy blue print fabric: two A strips (4½″ × 23″ each) and two B strips (28½″ × 4½″ each).

5. Take the A strips; fold under and press ¼″ on one long edge of each A strip to the wrong side of the fabric (Figure 6–1).

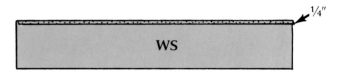

WS

¼″

6–1. *Press under a ¼″ seam allowance to the wrong side of each A strip on one long side.*

6. With a ½″ seam allowance, stitch one blue A strip on its unfolded long edge to one short side of the canvas rectangle; the *right* side of the blue strip should be against the *wrong* side of the canvas. Press along the seam line. Then press the blue A strip to the right side of the canvas (Figure 6–2). Repeat this with the second A strip on the other short side of the canvas.

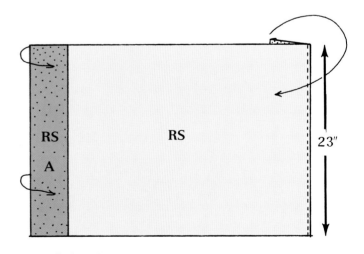

RS **A** **RS** 23″

6–2. Right: *Stitch an A strip on its unfolded long side to the wrong side of the canvas panel with ½″ seam allowance. The A strip's right side faces the back of the canvas.* **Left:** *The A strip is pressed around to the front of the canvas.*

7. Take the two navy B strips (28½″ × 4½″ each). Press under ¼″ on one long edge and both short edges to the wrong side of each strip (Figure 6-3).

6–3. Press under a ¼″ seam allowance to the wrong side of each B strip on one long and two short sides.

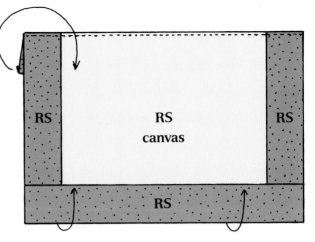

6–4. **Top:** *Stitch a B strip on its unfolded long side to the back of the canvas with ½″ seam allowance. The right side of the strip faces the wrong side of the canvas.* **Bottom:** *Press the B strip around to the right side of the canvas.*

8. With a ½″ seam allowance, stitch one B strip on its unfolded long edge to the long edge of the canvas, with the *right* side of the blue B strip against the *wrong* side of the canvas. Repeat with the second B strip. Press both strips along the seam line; then press the B strips to the front of the canvas (Figure 6-4).

9. Stitch along the A and B strips close to the fold in the turned-under hems (Figure 6-5) to secure the strips to the canvas front.

6–5. Stitch through the floor cloth close to the turned-under border hems to secure the border strips. The dashed lines are stitching lines. Machine appliqué the flowers and leaves, and machine embroider the stems in satin stitch.

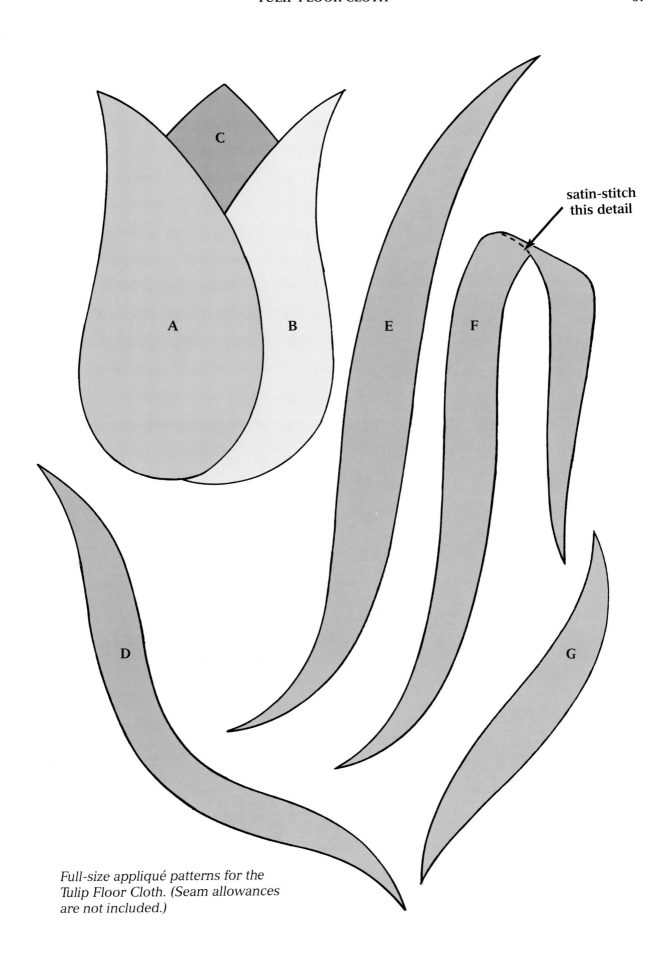

satin-stitch
this detail

C

A B E F

D G

*Full-size appliqué patterns for the
Tulip Floor Cloth. (Seam allowances
are not included.)*

10. Pin the flower pieces and leaves to the
    canvas front in a pleasing arrangement;
    refer to the color photograph for
    placement suggestions. The bottoms of the
    leaves should be between 1″ and 2″ up
    from the bottom blue B strip. Draw a stem
    line from the flower tops to the leaves (see
    Figure 6-5). Fuse the flowers and leaves to
    the front of the canvas.

11. Appliqué the flowers and leaves in place
    using all-purpose thread that matches
    each fabric piece. Embroider the flower
    stems in machine satin stitch with green
    thread (Figure 6-6).

12. Cut two 22″ lengths of fringe and secure
    the fringe to the wrong side of each short
    end of the floor cloth; either hand-stitch it
    in place or glue it (Figure 6-7).

13. Mark a line 1½″ out from the meeting of
    the canvas and the borders (Figure 6-8).
    Apply the satin ribbon along this line,
    "stitching in the ditch" along each side of
    the ribbon to secure it in place (see the
    "ditch" detail, Figure 6-9). This completes
    the floor cloth.

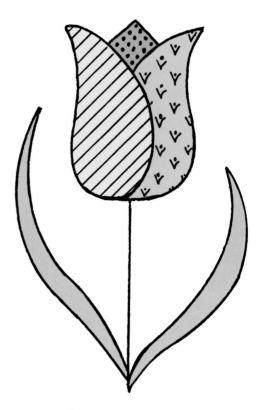

*6–6. Detail of the flower. Use a
different fabric for each of the three
flower sections. Satin-stitch the stem
lines.*

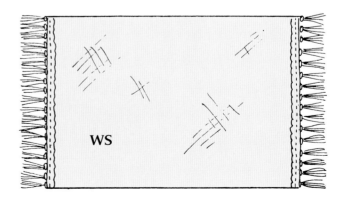

*6–7. Glue or hand-stitch the fringe to the
wrong side of the rug.*

6–8. Mark a line 1½″ out from the meeting of the canvas and the borders. Apply satin ribbon along the line.

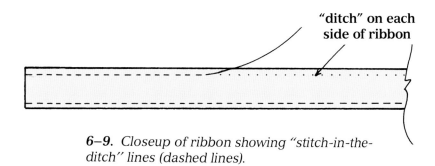

"ditch" on each side of ribbon

6–9. Closeup of ribbon showing "stitch-in-the-ditch" lines (dashed lines).

Straw Hat Wall Hanging

You can almost feel the breezes blowing the ribbons on these easy-to-stitch beauties! Finished size of wall hanging: 25″ × 29″. Finished block size: 8½″ × 10½″ (including ¼″ seam allowances).

Materials Required

- *⅓ yard light green print fabric for blocks*
- *¼ yard medium green print fabric for sashing*
- *½ yard floral print fabric for borders*
- *⅓ yard each of purple and pink fabric for bows and hatbands*
- *¼ yard each of 4 different tan or light-brown prints for the hats*
- *4 small white ribbon roses*
- *Threads to match the fabrics*
- *1½ yards of fusible fleece*
- *27″ × 31″ piece of backing fabric (your choice)*
- *27″ × 31″ piece of quilt batting*
- *4 yards of tan binding (2″ wide when opened; ½″-wide finished width)*

Directions

All seam allowances are ¼″ for piecing.

1. From the light green fabric, cut 4 rectangles, each 8½″ × 10½″.

2. Trace out the hat brim pattern from page 75 onto cardboard or template plastic. From *each* of the four tan and brown fabrics trace and cut out one hat brim.

3. From the fusible fleece, cut 4 hat brims *slightly* smaller (⅛″ all around) than the fabric brims. Fuse the fleece brims to the centers of the wrong sides of the fabric brims (Figure 7-1).

4. Trace out the appliqué pattern of the crown onto cardboard or template plastic. From each of the tan and brown fabrics, cut one crown (a total of 4 crowns).

5. From the fusible fleece, cut 4 crowns *slightly* smaller (⅛″) than the fabric crowns. Fuse the fleece crowns to the wrong sides of the fabric crowns (Figure 7-2a).

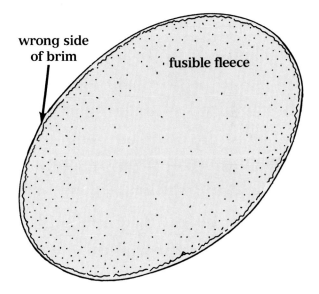

7–1. Fuse the fleece to the wrong side of the brim for each hat.

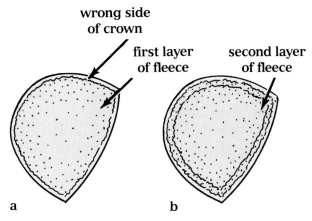

7–2. a: Fuse the first fleece crown to the wrong side of the fabric crown of each hat. b: Fuse the second (slightly smaller) fleece crown to the first fleece crown.

Closeup of hat block, showing quilting details.

6. From the fusible fleece, cut 4 crowns *slightly* smaller (⅛″) than the first set of fleece crowns; fuse them to the first set of fleece crowns (Figure 7-2b).

7. Place one brim on each light-green block, on a slight angle (see Figure 7-3). Pin them in place and machine appliqué the brims to the blocks with matching thread, using a medium-width satin stitch (about ¼″ wide).

8. For each hat, place the crown of the same tan fabric face-up on its corresponding brim and machine-appliqué it in place.

9. Trace out the hatband pattern from the appliqué pattern onto template plastic or cardboard and cut it out. Cut out two hatbands from purple fabric and two from pink fabric. Machine-appliqué a hatband to each hat with matching thread.

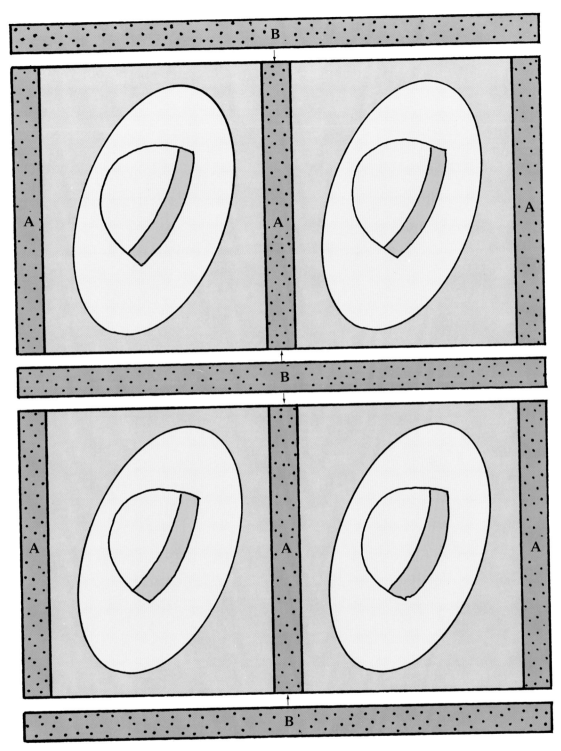

7–3. *Sew the A sashing strips between the blocks as shown. Then sew the B sashing strips as shown to complete the quilt center.*

10. From the medium-green fabric cut 6 A strips, each 1½″ × 10½″. Stitch 3 A strips, alternating with 2 hat blocks, to make a row, as shown in Figure 7-3. Make a second row the same way.

11. From the medium-green fabric, cut 3 B strips, each 1½″ × 19½″. Attach them above, between, and below the rows to make the quilt's center unit and press it (see Figure 7-3).

12. To make the outer borders, cut two C strips, 3½″ × 23½″ each, from the floral fabric; cut two D strips, 3½″ × 25½″, from the same fabric.

13. Stitch the strips to the quilt center, first joining the C strips to the sides as shown in Figure 7-4, and then adding the D strips. Stitching is done with right sides of fabric facing and ¼″ seam allowances. This completes the quilt top.

14. To join the three layers of the quilt before quilting, take the 27″ × 31″ piece of backing fabric. Lay the backing fabric face-down on your work surface, and center the quilt batting (27″ × 31″) over the backing. Last, center the quilt top over the batting. Pin-baste the layers together to prevent them from shifting during quilting. See the Basic Techniques chapter for further information on basting and quilting.

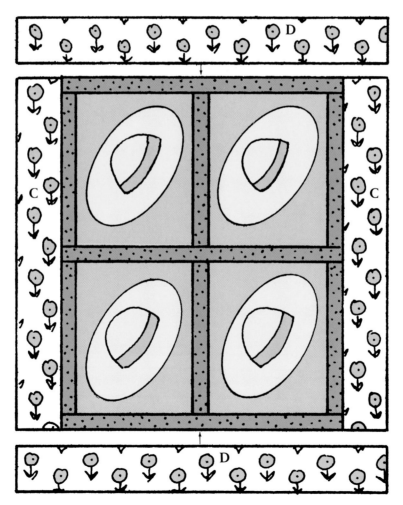

7–4. Attaching the floral borders. C borders are added first; then D borders.

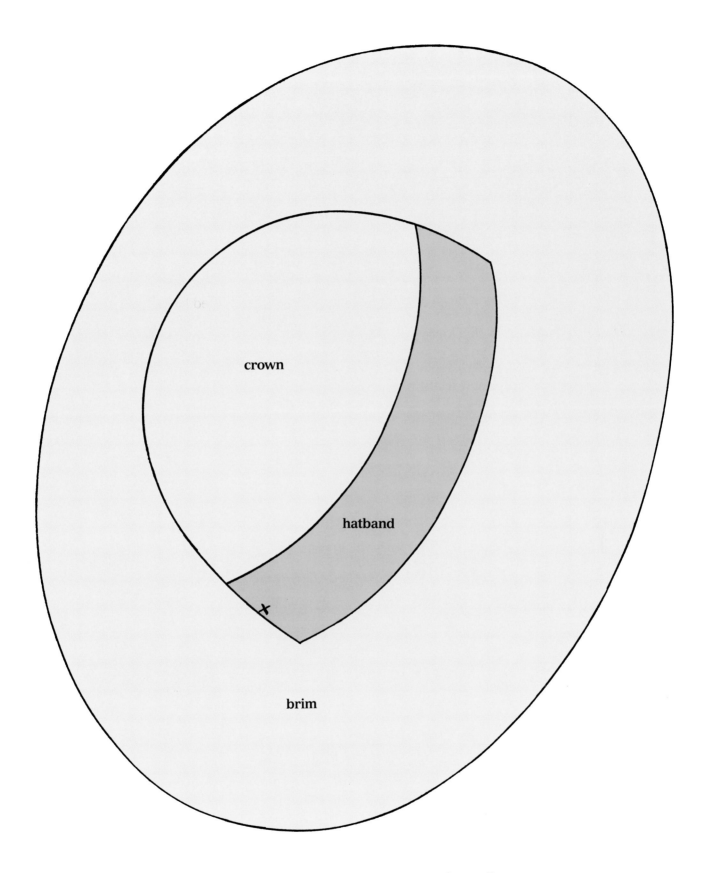

Full-size patterns for the hat brim, crown, and band. Seam allowances are not included.

15. Quilt the wall hanging as you desire, by hand or machine; see the closeup photo for guidance.

16. After quilting, baste close to the raw edges around the quilt top; then trim away the excess batting and backing fabric.

17. Bind the quilt with the bias binding, using thread to match the binding, and a ½″ seam allowance. (See the section on binding in the Basic Techniques chapter.)

18. To make the ties for the hats, cut two strips from the pink fabric and two strips from the purple fabric; each strip is 3″ × 24″. Fold each strip in half along its length with the right sides of the fabric together (Figure 7-5a). Stitch the strip along its short edges at an angle (Figure 7-5b), and stitch the long double edge closed, except for a 3″ opening at the center. Trim the ends of the strips as shown (Figure 7-5c). Turn the strips right-side out through the opening, and stitch the turning openings closed by hand.

19. Fold each strip in half and mark the center (Figure 7-6a). Make another mark 5″ from each side of the center mark (see Figure 7-6a). Fold each strip at the 5″ marks towards the center of the strip (Figure 7-6b).

20. Gather the center of the strip to form a bow (Figure 7-6c).

21. Hand-stitch one bow to each hat (Figure 7-7), where indicated by the "X" on the appliqué pattern.

22. Hand-stitch or glue one ribbon rose to the gathered area on each bow to complete the quilt.

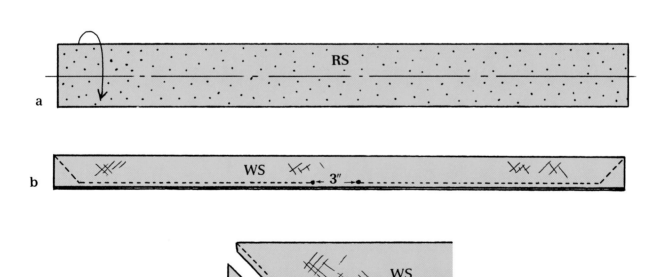

*7–5. Making the bows. **a:** Fold each 3″ × 24″ strip in half on its length.*
***b:** Stitch on its open long edge, and stitch the ends at an angle. Leave a 3″ opening for turning. **c:** Trim the bow ends as shown.*

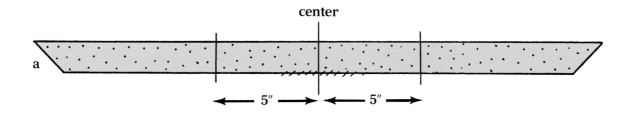

center

a

← 5″ → ← 5″ →

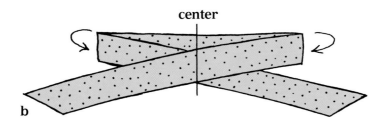

center

b

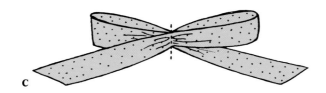

c

*7–6. Folding the bows. **a:** Mark the center; then mark 5″ out from the center on each side. **b:** Fold the strip along the 2 outer markings, crossing the ties at the center. **c:** Gather the ties along the center to form the bow.*

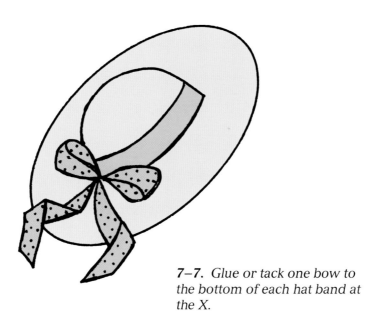

7–7. Glue or tack one bow to the bottom of each hat band at the X.

Pieced Pillow Sham

This sham works up quickly and adds a dainty touch to any bedroom. The sham fits the "sham pillows" available in department stores; however, you can substitute a queen-size pillow if needed. Finished outer size of sham: approximately 34″ × 28″; finished size of pillow pocket: 28″ × 22″.

Materials Required

- *1 yard floral print fabric*
- *¾ yard natural-colored fabric*
- *½ yard terra cotta pink fabric*
- *¼ yard green fabric*
- *All-purpose threads to match the fabrics*
- *35″ × 29″ piece of fleece*
- *35″ × 29″ piece of muslin*

Directions

All seam allowances are ¼″.

1. From the natural-colored fabric, cut one rectangle 16½″ × 22½″ and two strips, 2½″ × 36″ each. Set the rectangles aside for the center panels.

2. Cut one 2½″ × 36″ strip from the terra cotta pink fabric.

3. Stitch one natural-colored strip to each long side of the terra cotta pink strip (Figure 8-1). Press the resulting 3-band strip. Cut the strip into 12 units, each 2½″ long; these will be A units; discard the excess.

4. From the terra cotta pink fabric, cut two strips, 2½″ × 18″ each. Cut one strip the same size from the floral print fabric. Stitch the pink strips to each side of the floral strip and press. Cut the strip into 6 units, each 2½″ long; these are the B units (Figure 8-2).

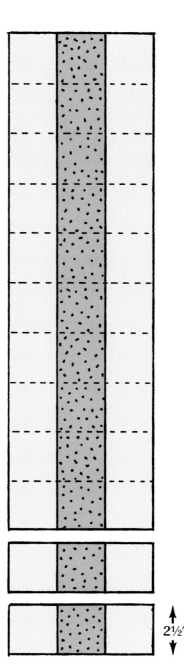

8–1. *Three strips (natural–terra cotta pink–natural) joined and then cut into 2½″-long A units.*

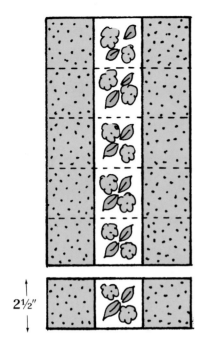

2½"

8–2. B units, formed from three joined strips (terra cotta pink–floral– terra cotta) that are cut into 2½"-long pieces.

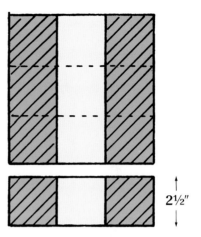

2½"

8–3. C units, formed from three joined strips (green–natural– green), cut into 2½"- long pieces.

5. From the green fabric, cut two strips, 2½" × 12" each. Cut a strip the same size from the natural-colored fabric. With the natural strip in the center stitch the strips together on their long sides and press (Figure 8-3). Cut the strip into 4 units, each 2½" long; these are the C units.

6. Stitch an A unit above a B unit and one below the B unit to make a nine-patch flower block (see Figure 8-4). Repeat this 5 more times to make a total of six.

A unit

+

B unit

=

9-patch flower block

+

A unit

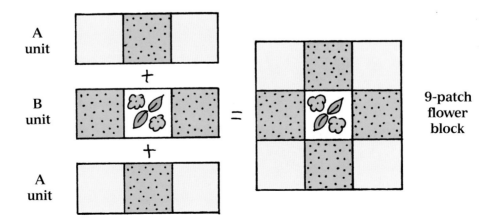

8–4. A 9-patch flower block, formed from 2 A units and a B unit.

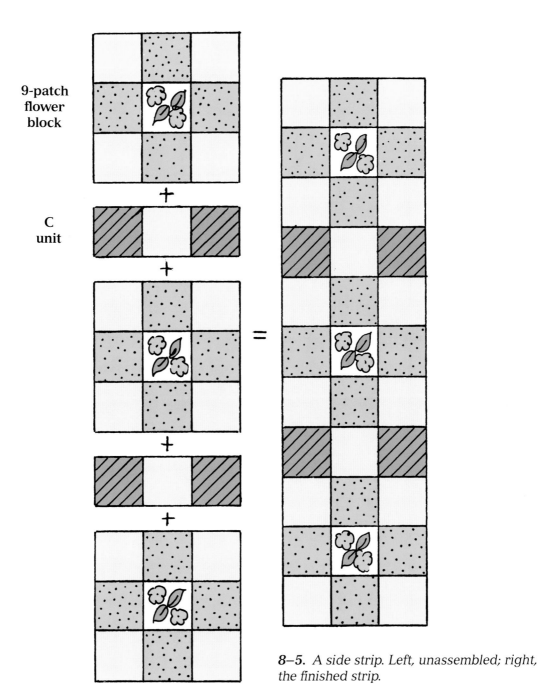

9-patch
flower
block

C
unit

8–5. A side strip. Left, unassembled; right,
the finished strip.

7. As shown in Figure 8-5, join 9-patch
flower blocks, alternating with C units, to
make a side strip of 3 blocks and 2 C units.
Make another side strip the same way.

8. Stitch a side strip to each long edge of a
natural-colored rectangle cut in Step 1
(Figure 8-5).

9. From the floral print fabric, cut 4 D strips,
3½″ × 28½″ each. Stitch one D strip to the
top and bottom of the sham center. Stitch
the remaining 2 D strips to the sides of the
sham center (Figure 8-7). Press the
completed sham front.

10. Tape the 35″ × 29″ piece of muslin on a flat

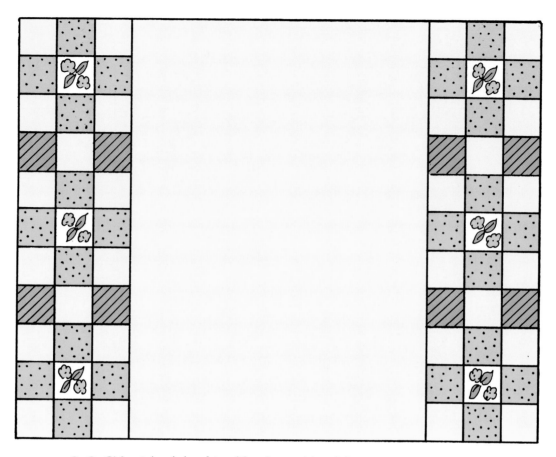

8–6. Side strips joined to either long side of the natural-colored center.

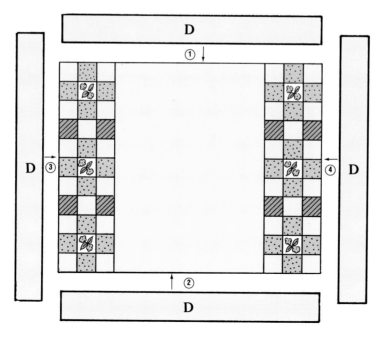

8–7. Join floral D strips to the sham center.
Circled numbers indicate order of piecing.

surface with masking tape. Center the 35″ × 29″ fleece over the muslin; center the sham front, right-side up, over the fleece. Pin-baste the layers together to keep them from shifting, remove the tape, and quilt the sham front as you desire. After quilting, trim away the excess fleece and muslin. (See the Basic Techniques chapter for basting and quilting instructions.)

11. From the floral print fabric cut two rectangles, each 20½″ × 28½″. Hem one long side of each piece by turning under ¼″ to the wrong side and turning under ¼″ again; stitch the hem down to secure it (Figure 8-8). Press the piece.

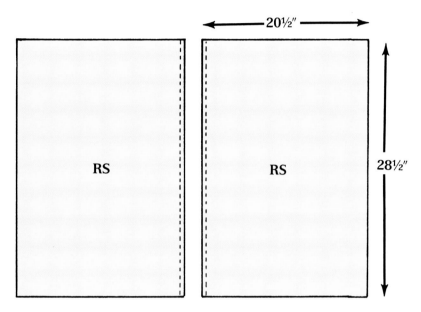

8–8. Hem one long edge of each backing piece.

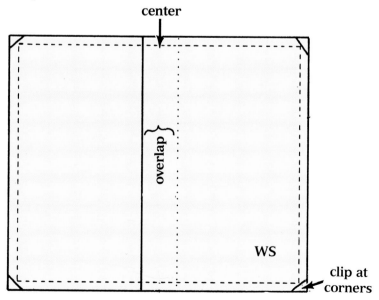

8–9. Overlap the backing pieces, wrong-side up, over the right-side up pillow sham top. Stitch with ¼″ seam allowance around the edges.

12. Place the sham front face-up on a flat surface. Place the two rectangles from Step 11 face-down on the sham front, having the hemmed edges overlapping at the center of the sham. This leaves an opening through which to insert the pillow, eventually. Stitch around the edges of the sham with a ¼″ seam allowance (Figure 8-9). Clip the corners of the seam allowances and turn the sham right-side out through the overlapped opening.

13. Press the sham. Pin the layers of the sham together in the floral border area to keep the layers from shifting. Stitch "in the ditch" around the inner border seam where it meets the central panel; stitch ¼″ from the outside edges of the sham also (Figure 8-10). The sham will now have a flanged border. The inner section is the pillow pocket.

14. Insert the pillow through the overlapped opening.

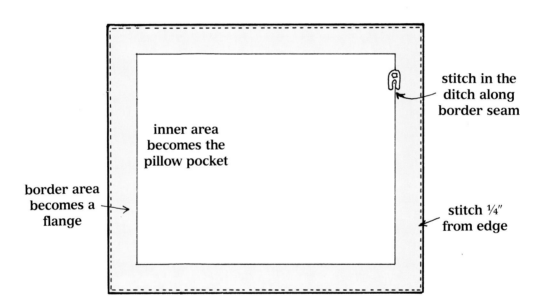

8–10. Stitch in the ditch along the border seam to make the pillow's flanged border. Stitch ¼″ from the outer edge of the border also.

Catch of the Day Lap Quilt

The bright colors and fish design make this an ideal quilt for someone who loves the outdoors. When stitched and quilted by machine, this quilt is sturdy enough to take on any adventure! This quilt uses rotary cutting methods, but you can use scissors if you prefer. Finished size of a block: 24½″ × 15½″ (including ¼″ seam allowances). Finished size of quilt: 69″ × 69″.

Materials Required

- *1½ yards light blue fabric (blue print in model)*
- *1½ yards yellow fabric (yellow print in model)*
- *1 yard black fabric (black print in model)*
- *¾ yard red fabric*
- *⅔ yard green fabric (green print in model)*
- *8 yards of green bias binding (2" wide when opened; ½" wide when finished)*
- *72" × 72" piece of quilt batting*
- *72" × 72" piece of solid green fabric for backing*
- *All-purpose threads to match fabrics*

9–1. A fish block, showing colors of pieces and rows.

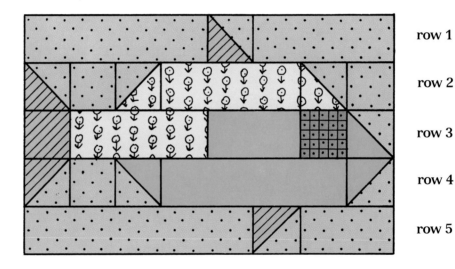

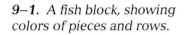

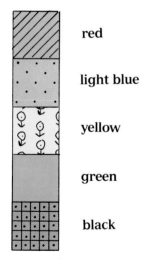

red

light blue

yellow

green

black

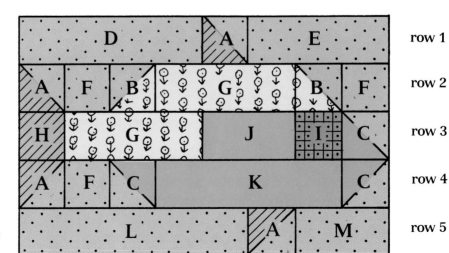

9–2. The fish block, showing unit and piece labels.

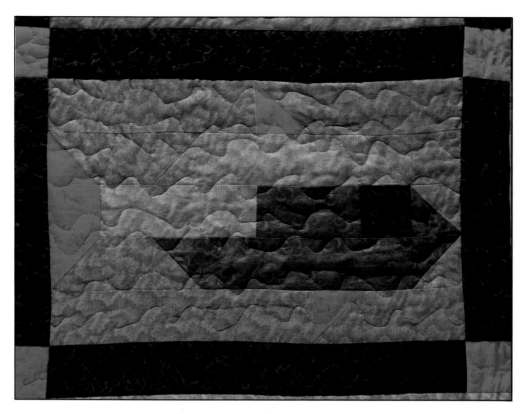

Closeup of a fish block, showing piecing and quilting details.

Directions

Overview: All seam allowances are ¼" unless otherwise noted. The quilt consists of six rectangular fish blocks, separated by sashing, with a border around them. Each fish block is made up of 5 pieced rows, which in turn are made up of various pieced units and strips. We will make the units and strips first, and then assemble them in blocks (Figure 9-1 and 9-2).

Row 1

1. For Row 1 of the blocks: From the blue and the red fabrics, cut one 13" × 17" rectangle of each. Place the rectangles together, with right sides facing. Mark off twelve 3⅞" × 3⅞" squares onto the wrong side of one rectangle. Mark a diagonal line through each square to divide it into triangles (Figure 9-3), but don't cut anything. Pin the two rectangles together.

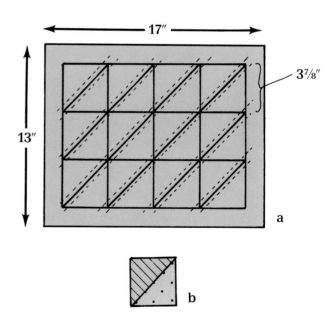

9–3. a: *Making the pieced A units; stitch on either side of the diagonal lines; then cut.* **b:** *The finished Unit A for Row 1.*

Using a ¼″ seam allowance, stitch along only one side of each diagonal line. Then stitch along the other side of each diagonal line, as shown in Figure 9-3.

2. Cut the triangles apart along the marked lines. Open each triangle out to form a pieced square, Unit A (Figure 9-3b). You will have 24 of Unit A. Set them aside for now.

3. From the light blue fabric cut 6 D strips, 3½″ × 12½″ each. Also cut 6E strips, 3½″ × 9½″, from the light blue fabric.

4. Stitch one D strip to an A Unit and add an E strip to form Row 1, as shown in Figure 9-4. Repeat this 5 times for a total of six of Row 1. (The remaining A Units will be used in rows 2, 4 and 5.)

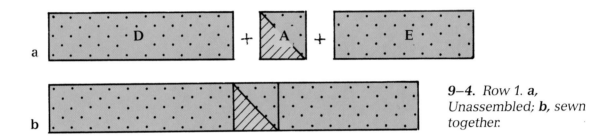

a

b

*9–4. Row 1. **a**, Unassembled; **b**, sewn together.*

Row 2

5. To begin Row 2 of the blocks: cut a 9″ × 13″ rectangle from the yellow fabric and one from the light blue fabric. Mark six 3⅞″ squares on the wrong side of one of the rectangles. Draw diagonal lines in each square. Place the yellow and blue rectangles together with right sides facing and stitch ¼″ from either side of the diagonals as you did to make the A Units in row 1 (Figure 9-5a). Cut the triangles apart on the marked lines and open each out to form a pieced square, Unit B (Figure 9-5b). You will have 12 of Unit B. Set them aside.

6. From the light blue fabric cut 12 3½″ × 3½″ F squares. Set them aside.

7. From the yellow fabric, cut 12 G strips 3½″ × 9½″ each. (Set aside 6 for Row 3.)

8. To piece Row 2 of the blocks, see Figure 9-6, and join the various squares, strips, and pieced squares as shown. Make 5 more of Row 2 in the same way. Set them aside.

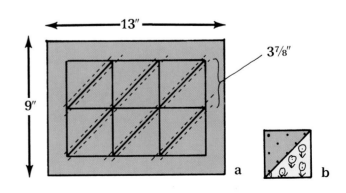

*9–5. Making the pieced B units. **a**: Stitch on either side of the diagonal lines; then cut. **b**: The finished Unit B for Row 2.*

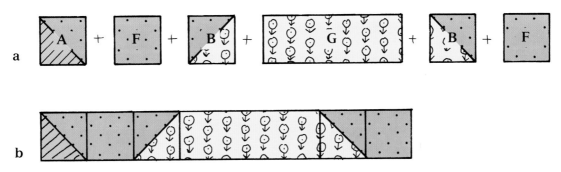

9–6. Piecing Row 2. **a:** *The unassembled pieces in order.* **b:** *The completed row.*

Row 3

9. To begin Row 3 of the blocks, we'll first make the Unit C squares. Cut a 5″ × 13″ rectangle from green fabric and one from light blue fabric the same size. Mark three 3⅞″ squares on the wrong side of one of the rectangles (Figure 9-7a). Mark the diagonals on the squares, as shown in 9-7a. Pin the green fabric and blue fabric rectangles together with right sides facing and stitch them ¼″ from the diagonals, as you did for the pieced squares made earlier (e.g., Unit A). Cut the triangles apart on the marked lines. Open each out to make a Unit C pieced square (see Figure 9-7b). You will have 6 of Unit C. Set them aside for now.

10. Cut six 3½″ × 3½″ H squares from red fabric. Cut six 3½″ × 3½″ I squares from black fabric. Cut six 3½″ × 6½″ J strips from green fabric.

11. To piece Row 3, join the strips, squares, and pieced Unit C as shown in Figure 9-8. Repeat for a total of six of Row 3. Press the rows.

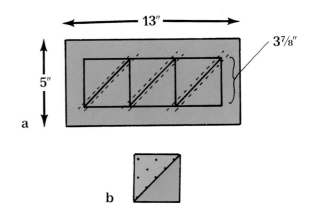

9–7. **a:** *Making the pieced C units for Row 3.* **b:** *The finished Unit C.*

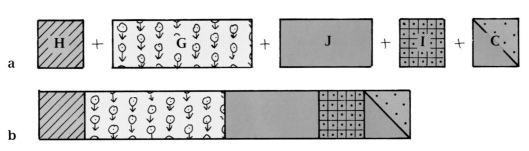

9–8. Row 3. **a:** *Unassembled.* **b:** *Sewn together.*

Row 4

12. To begin Row 4, first cut a 9″ × 13″ rectangle from light blue fabric and one the same size from green fabric. On the wrong side of one rectangle, mark six 3⅞″ squares as shown in Figure 9-9a. Mark the diagonals. Pin the two rectangles together with right sides facing. Stitch on either side of the diagonal, cut the triangle units apart; open them out, and press them as you did for Unit A and the other pieced units. Each blue + green pieced square is a Unit C. You will have 12 of them.

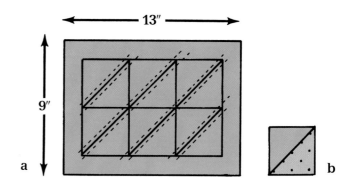

9–9. a: *Making the pieced C units for Row 4.* **b:** *The finished Unit C.*

13. Also for Row 4, cut six 3½″ × 3½″ F squares from light blue fabric. Cut six 3½″ × 12½″ K strips from green fabric. Assemble Row 4 as shown in Figure 9-10a. Make five more of Row 4. Press them.

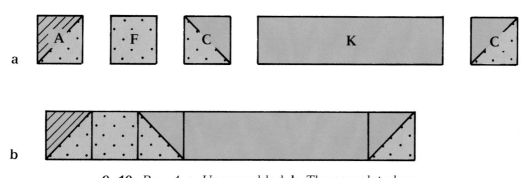

9–10. *Row 4.* **a:** *Unassembled.* **b:** *The completed row.*

Row 5

14. From light blue fabric, cut six L strips, 3½″ × 15½″, and six M strips, 3½″ × 6½″. To assemble Row 5, join an L strip to Unit A, and join strip M on the other side (see Figure 9-11a). Repeat five more times to make a total of six of Row 5. Press them.

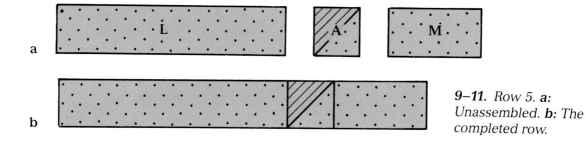

9–11. *Row 5.* **a:** *Unassembled.* **b:** *The completed row.*

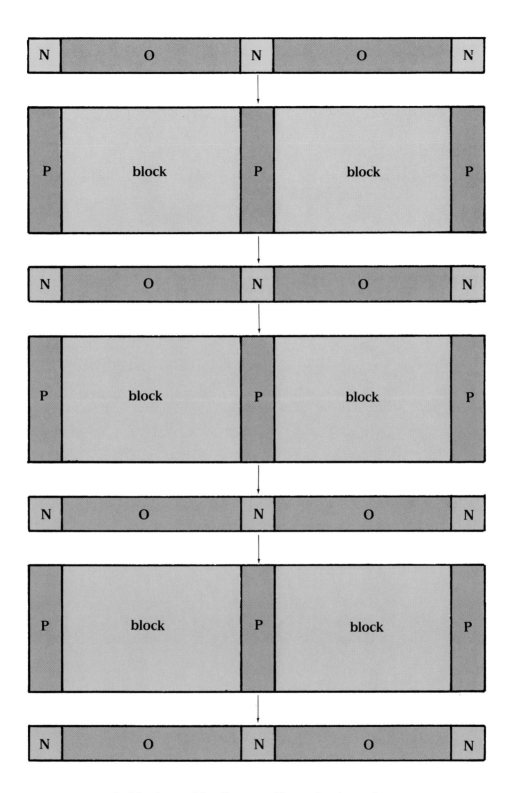

9–12. *Assembly diagram.* **Top:** *a horizontal sashing strip (N-O-N-O-N) is joined to a pieced block row by seaming the two together. Repeat to assemble the rest of the quilt center.*

Assembling the Blocks

15. Lay out each block in rows. Double-check their orientation (see Figures 9-1 and 9-2). Pin Row 1 to Row 2 with right sides facing, and seam them together, being sure the ends align. Continue to stitch the rest of the rows together in the same way.

16. Repeat the joining of rows (Step 15) with all the rows for each block, until you have assembled all 6 blocks.

Sashing and Quilt Center Assembly

17. To make the sashing squares and strips: Cut twelve 3½″ × 3½″ N squares from red fabric. Cut eight 3½″ × 24½″ O strips from black fabric. To make a horizontal sashing strip (Figure 9-12, top) stitch red N squares alternating with black O strips, as shown. Make a total of 4 horizontal sashing strips. Set them aside.

18. From black fabric, cut 9 vertical P sashing strips, 3½″ × 15½″ each.

19. Make a row of 3 P strips and 2 fish blocks by stitching them together as shown in Figure 9-12. Make 2 more rows the same way.

20. Assemble the quilt center by stitching the horizontal sashing above, between and below the block rows (see Figure 9-12). Press the assembled unit.

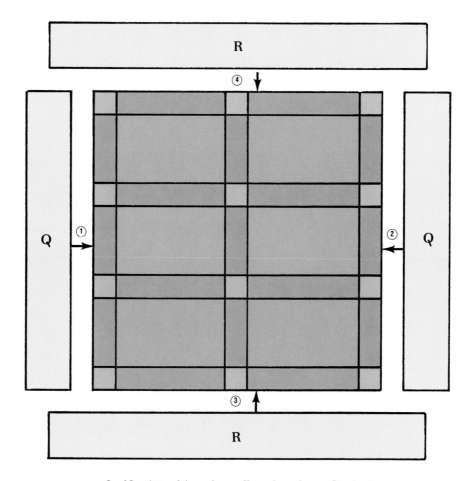

9–13. Attaching the yellow borders. Circled numbers indicate the order of assembly.

Borders and Quilting

21. For the side borders, cut two yellow Q strips, 6½″ × 57½″ each, and stitch them to the sides of the quilt center (Figure 9-13). Cut two yellow R strips, 6½″ × 69½″ each, and stitch them to the top and bottom of the quilt. Press the unit.

22. Lay the 72″ × 72″ backing fabric face-down on a clean floor and tape it at the corners to secure it to the floor. Center the 72″ × 72″ batting over the backing. Center the quilt top, face-up, over the batting.

23. Pin-baste the layers together to keep them from shifting during quilting: start at the center of the quilt and work your way outwards, smoothing the fabric as you pin.

24. Quilt the quilt as desired by hand or machine. (See the Basic Techniques Chapter and the closeup photo for quilting information.) Then baste around the outside of the quilt top, close to the raw edges, and trim away any excess batting and backing.

25. Bind the quilt with the binding, using thread to match. (See the binding instructions in the Basic Techniques chapter.)

Doily-Trimmed Flower Pillows

Inexpensive dime-store doilies or old ones from your own collection can be used on this romantic trio. Try using different shapes and sizes if you'd like; finished size of pillows: blue pillow, 16″ × 16″; purple pillow, 14″ × 14″; pink pillow, 14″ diameter.

Materials Required

Blue Pillow

- *2 squares of blue fabric, 17″ × 17″ each (blue print in model)*
- *6″-diameter round lace doily*
- *Scraps of green, pink, purple and yellow fabrics*
- *17″ × 17″ piece of fusible webbing*
- *All-purpose threads to match fabrics*
- *16″ × 16″ pillow form*
- *2 yards white corded piping*

Purple Pillow

- *2 squares of purple fabric, 15″ × 15″ each (purple print in model)*
- *10″-square doily*
- *Scraps of pink, yellow, and green fabrics*
- *7″ × 7″ piece of fusible webbing*
- *All-purpose threads to match fabrics*
- *14″ × 14″ pillow form*
- *2 yards white corded piping*

Pink Pillow

- *2 squares of pink fabric, 15″ × 15″ each (pink print in model)*
- *8″-square doily*
- *Scraps of yellow fabric (yellow print in model) and green fabric*
- *10″ × 10″ piece of fusible webbing*
- *All-purpose threads to match fabrics*
- *2 yards of 3″-wide pregathered lace edging*
- *14″-diameter pillow form*

Directions

Blue Pillow

1. Fold one of the 17″ blue squares into quarters to mark the center and press it. Open the square. It will be the pillow top. (Set aside the second square for the backing.) Lay the doily in the center of the creased square on the right side of the fabric and pin it in place.

2. From the appliqué patterns on page 96, trace out the leaf, petal, and circles onto cardboard or template plastic and cut them out.

3. Trace 8 leaves, 8 petals, 1 inner circle, and 1 outer circle onto the paper side of fusible webbing, using the templates. Cut out the webbing shapes.

4. Fuse the webbing petals to the wrong side of pink scrap fabric. Cut out the petals and place them around the doily on the pillow top, tucking the raw inner edges of the petals under the doily to conceal them (Figure 10-1). Fuse the petals in place.

10–1. *Blue pillow top showing placement of petals, leaves, and circles. Place the petal ends under the doily before fusing the petals.*

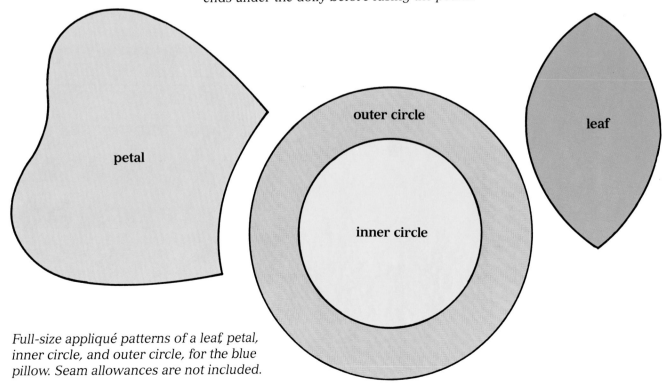

Full-size appliqué patterns of a leaf, petal, inner circle, and outer circle, for the blue pillow. Seam allowances are not included.

Closeup of the blue pillow, showing appliqué details.

5. Fuse the webbing leaves to the back of the green scrap fabrics and cut them out. Fuse 2 leaves to the pillow top at the corners, as shown in Figure 10-1, close to the flower petals.

6. Fuse the webbing inner circle to the wrong side of the yellow fabric. Fuse the webbing outer circle to the wrong side of the purple scrap fabric. Cut them both out. Fuse the purple circle to the center of the doily on the pillow top. Fuse the yellow inner circle to the center of the outer circle on the pillow top.

7. Machine-appliqué all of the appliqué pieces in place with matching threads, using a medium-width machine satin stitch. Secure the loose edges of the doily, taking small hand stitches with a needle and white thread.

8. Baste the piping around the edges of the pillow top, so that the raw edges of the piping are even with the raw edges of the pillow top. See the Basic Techniques chapter for more information on piping.

9. Place the 17″ square backing fabric and the pillow top together with their right sides

facing. Stitch the backing to the pillow top along the sides, leaving a 10″ turning opening along the center of the fourth side. Clip the corners of the seam allowance and turn the pillow cover right-side out. Press it.

10. Insert the 16″ pillow form and hand-stitch the opening closed.

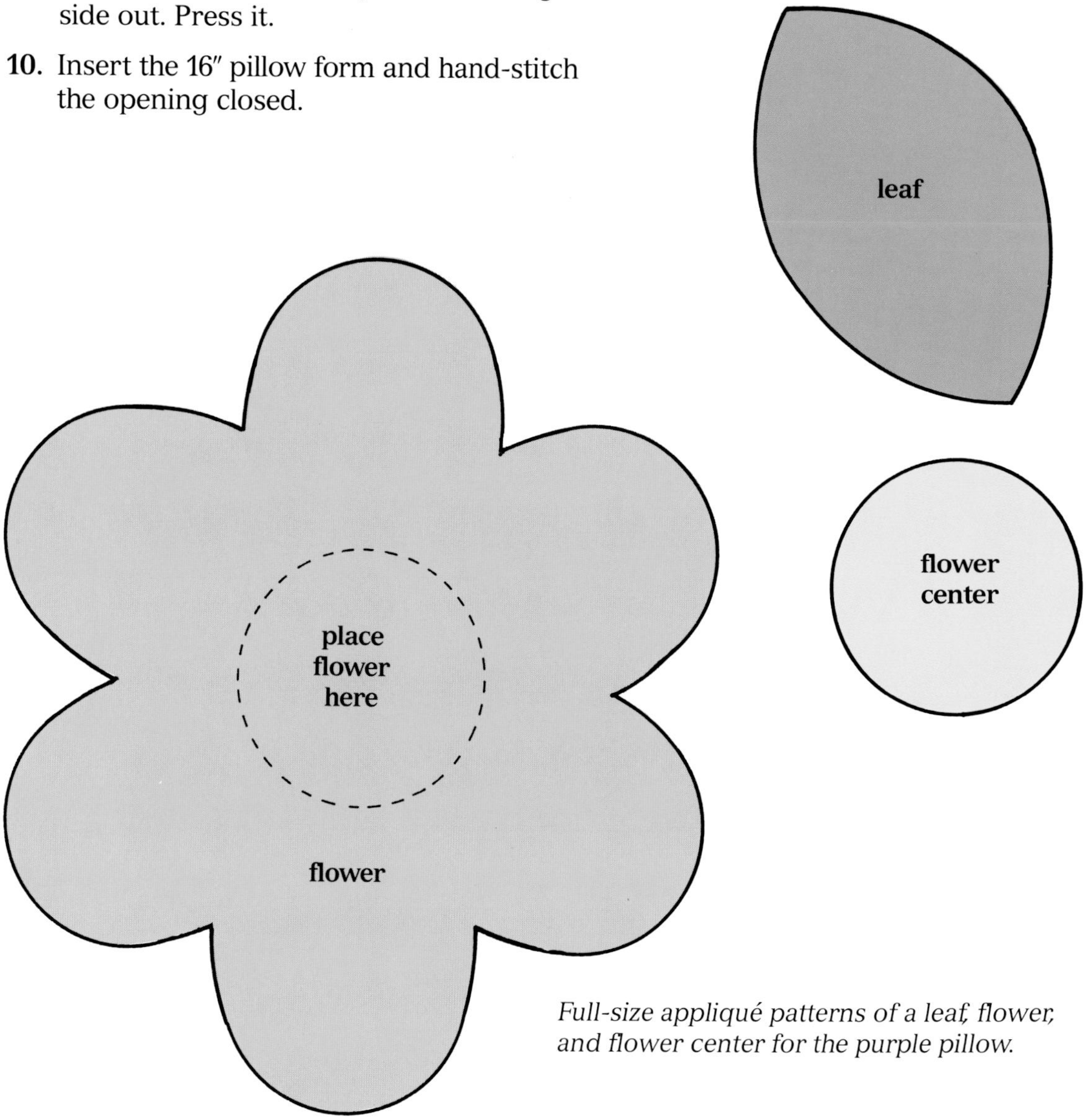

leaf

flower center

place flower here

flower

Full-size appliqué patterns of a leaf, flower, and flower center for the purple pillow.

Purple Pillow

1. Fold one of the 15″ purple squares into quarters and press it to mark the center. (Set aside the second purple square for the pillow backing.)

2. From the appliqué patterns above, trace out the leaf, flower, and flower center onto cardboard or template plastic and cut them out.

10–2. Purple pillow, showing the position of flower, leaves, and doily.

3. Trace one flower, one flower center, and two leaves onto the paper side of fusible webbing, and cut them out. Fuse the flower to the wrong side of the pink fabric; fuse the leaves to the wrong side of the green fabric; fuse the flower center to the wrong side of the yellow scrap fabric. Cut out all of the shapes.

4. Center the doily on the creased purple square and pin it in place. Secure the doily to the purple square by taking small stitches by hand with a needle and white sewing thread to anchor it.

5. Center the pink flower on the doily and fuse it in place (Figure 10-2). Place the flower center on the flower and the leaves beside the flower and fuse them in place. Machine-appliqué the pieces in place as you did for the blue pillow.

6. Baste the piping to the outer edges of the pillow top as you did for the blue pillow. (See the Basic Techniques chapter for more information on piping.)

7. Stitch the purple backing piece (15″ × 15″) to the pillow front, right sides facing, along all 4 edges, leaving a 10″ opening along the fourth side for turning. Clip the corners of the seam allowances and turn the pillow cover right-side out. Press it.

8. Insert the 14″ pillow form into the pillow cover. Hand-stitch the opening closed.

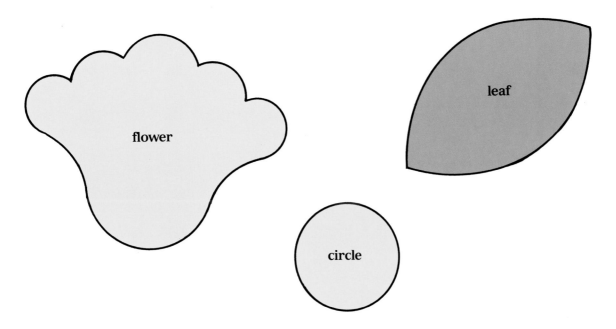

Full-size appliqué patterns of a flower, leaf, and circle, for the pink pillow.

Pink Pillow

1. Fold one of the pink 15″ squares into quarters and press it to mark the center. Trim the square into a 15″-diameter circle. Using the circle as a pattern, trim the second square into a circle for the pillow back.

2. Center the doily on the right side of the creased pink circle. Pin it in place; then secure the doily to the pink circle by hand, using white thread and a needle.

3. From the appliqué patterns above, trace the leaf, flower, and flower center onto cardboard or template plastic and cut them out.

4. Trace 4 flowers, 8 leaves and one circle onto the paper side of fusible webbing and cut them out. Fuse the webbing flowers to the wrong side of the yellow fabric. Fuse the webbing leaves to the wrong side of the green fabrics; fuse the webbing circle to the

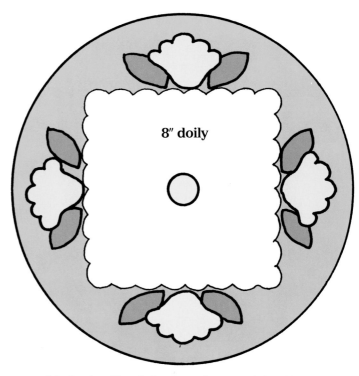

10–3. Appliqué diagram for the pink pillow.

wrong side of the yellow fabric. Cut out all the shapes from the fabrics. Fuse the leaves and flowers in place around the doily, and fuse the flower center in place on the doily center (see Figure 10-3).

5. Machine appliqué the pieces in place as you did for the appliqués on the blue pillow.

6. Baste the lace edging to the edges of the appliquéd circle on its right side, having the gathered raw edge of the lace even with the raw edges of the circle (Figure 10-4).

7. Take the undecorated circle cut in Step 1 and the appliquéd circle. Pin them together with right sides facing and stitch them together around the edges with ¼″ seam allowances; leave a 10″ opening unstitched so you can turn the pillow cover. Clip the seam allowances (Figure 10-5) and turn the pillow cover right-side out. Insert the pillow form and hand-stitch the opening closed.

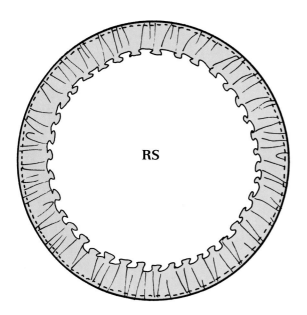

10–4. Round pillow: Baste the gathered lace around the right side of the pillow top, with raw edges even.

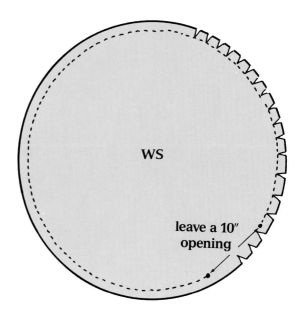

10–5. Clip the seam allowances of the pillow top all around the pillow.

Child's Gardening Apron and Tote Bag

Let them get this set as dirty as they want—it's machine washable, of course! Finished size of apron: about 22″ × 24″. Finished size of tote: 13″ × 14″, excluding the handles.

Materials Required for the Set

- *2 yards "gardening print" fabric or floral fabric (see photo)*
- *2 yards natural-colored fabric (for backing and lining)*
- *Scraps of purple, green, yellow, and red solid-colored fabrics*
- *½ yard white fabric*
- *1 yard fusible webbing*
- *All purpose threads to match the fabrics*
- *6 yards of green extra-wide double-fold bias binding (2" wide opened; ½" wide, finished size)*
- *44" × 36" piece of fleece or quilt batting*

Directions

Gardening Apron

1. Cut one 22" × 24" rectangle from the gardening print fabric and one the same size from the natural-colored fabric. Enlarge the grid pattern for the apron (page 109). Cut the apron shape from the print fabric rectangle and the natural-colored rectangle.

2. From the white fabric, cut one 22" × 13" rectangle. Fold the rectangle in half to 6½" × 22" and press it (Figure 11-1a). Then fold the resulting double-layered strip into thirds and press it again (Figure 11-1B). Mark along the crease lines with washable pen to form the pocket division lines.

3. Trace out the appliqué patterns on page 108 onto cardboard or template plastic and cut them out. Mark the top sides.

4. Trace the reversed appliqué patterns onto the paper side of fusible webbing and cut them out of the webbing. Fuse the appliqués to the wrong sides of their respective fabrics; the fabric color is indicated on the patterns.

5. Also trace the appliqué patterns onto the apron pocket divisions, making sure the apron pocket's folded edge is on top and the double raw edge of the fabric is at the bottom. Transfer all of the markings to the pocket panel with washable pen or pencil (Figure 11-2).

6. Appliqué the pieces to the pocket divisions, using threads that match the fabrics and a medium-width machine satin-stitch. See the Basic Techniques chapter for appliqué instructions. Then narrow the width of the satin stitch to approximately ⅛" and stitch along the tendril (curly) lines and the leaf lines with green thread. Stitch along the radish lines with red thread (see appliqué pattern).

7. Place the print apron panel and the solid apron panel together with the *wrong* sides facing and the print side up. Baste around the edges, ⅛" in from the edges. Place the pocket panel along the bottom edge of the apron, so that the raw edges of the panel

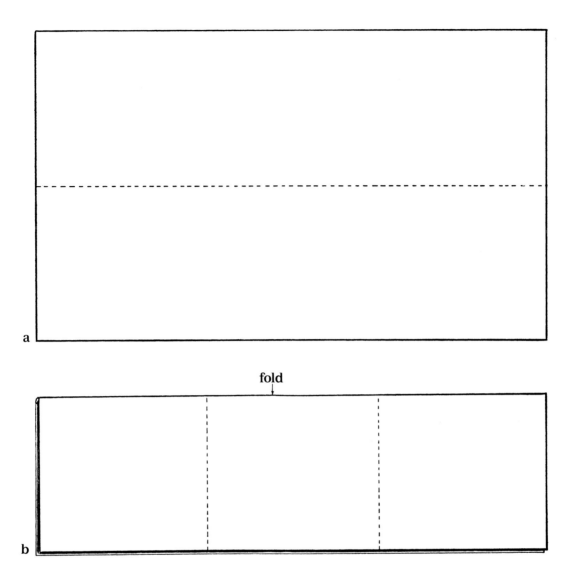

11–1. *Making the pocket.* **a:** *Fold the white 22″ × 13″ rectangle in half to 6½″ × 22″ and press it.* **b:** *Fold the doubled white rectangle into thirds and mark the pocket lines of the apron.*

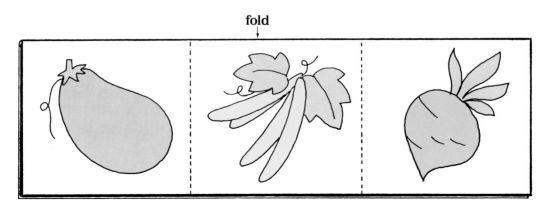

11–2. *Appliqué patterns, transferred to the apron pocket. Folded edge is up.*

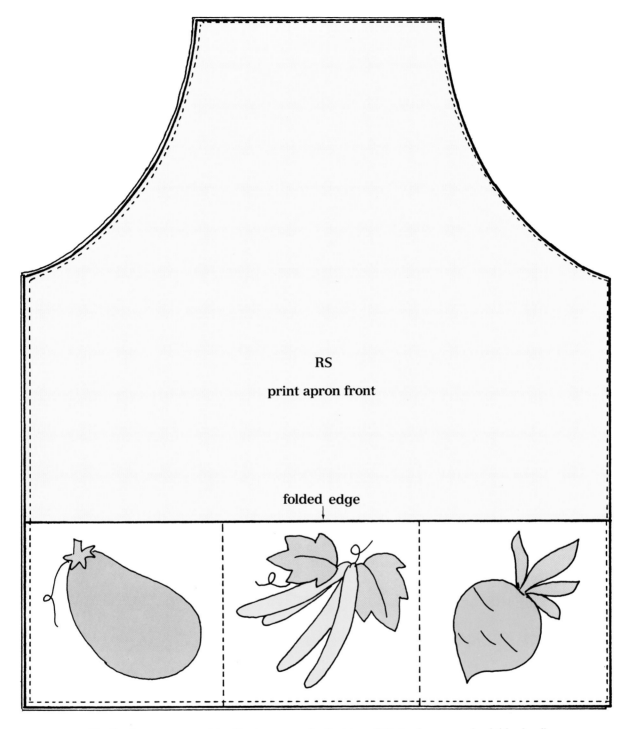

RS

print apron front

folded edge

11–3. Apron assembly. Baste around all sides. Stitch along marked (dashed) lines to make the pockets, using white thread.

are even with the raw edges of the apron. Machine-stitch along the marked pocket lines with white thread to make the pocket divisions (Figure 11-3).

8. Using the green bias binding, bind the top edge of the apron; bind the sides and bottom of the apron starting just below one armhole and finishing just before

the other (Figure 11-4). See the Basic Techniques chapter for binding information.

9. Cut the remaining binding into two equal lengths. Fold each length in half to find the center and mark the center with a pin. Open the binding and place one long raw edge along the armhole of the apron on the back side, centering the binding at the center of the armhole (Figure 11-5). Stitch the binding to the armhole edge in the crease of the binding that is closest to the apron's raw edge (Figure 11-6). Repeat for the second armhole.

10. Fold the loose edge of the binding over to the front side of the apron. Stitch along the *entire* length of the bias tape, starting at the short end of one tail of the binding, stitching along its length to form a tie, then continuing to stitch along the armhole, and then stitching along the rest of the length of binding that forms the other end of the tie (Figure 11-7). Repeat this for the second armhole. This completes the apron.

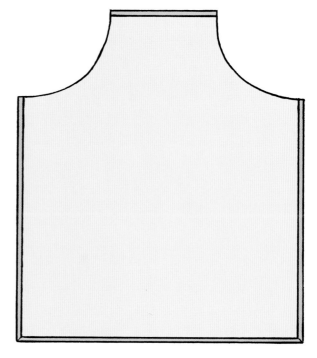

11–4. Bind the top and sides of the apron (not the armholes).

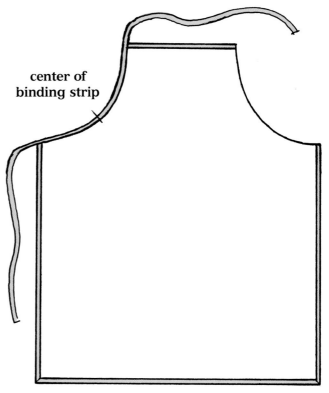

11–5. Center each strip of binding on the center of the armhole.

center of
binding strip

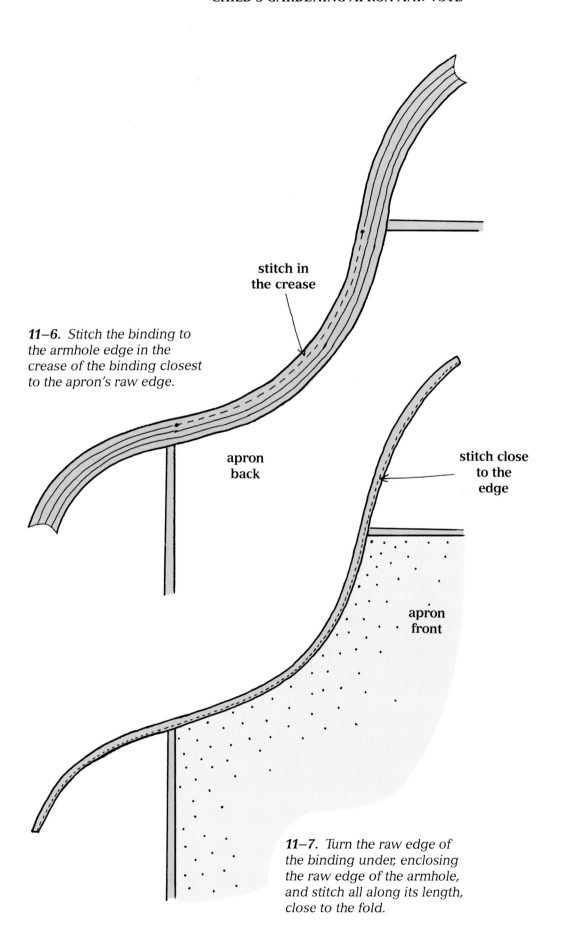

stitch in the crease

11–6. *Stitch the binding to the armhole edge in the crease of the binding closest to the apron's raw edge.*

apron back

stitch close to the edge

apron front

11–7. *Turn the raw edge of the binding under, enclosing the raw edge of the armhole, and stitch all along its length, close to the fold.*

Full-size appliqué patterns for the apron. Seam allowances are not included.

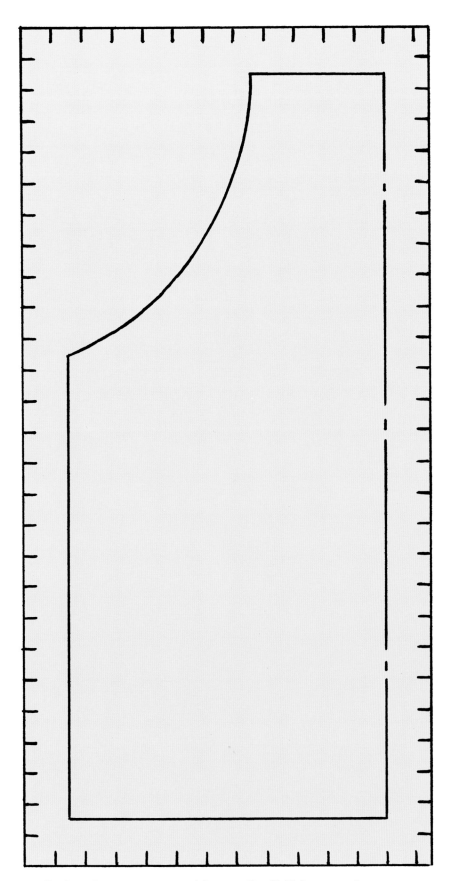

Reduced apron pattern, 1 box = 1″ × 1″. Enlarge and trace out pattern. (See the Basic Techniques chapter for information on enlarging a pattern.)

Tote Bag

1. Cut one 7½″ × 8½″ rectangle of white fabric.

2. Trace and cut out the appliqué patterns given below onto cardboard or template plastic. Mark the top of the patterns.

3. Trace the reversed appliqué patterns onto the paper side of fusible webbing, and cut them out of the webbing.

4. Fuse each webbing appliqué to the wrong side of the correct-colored fabric (see the appliqué pattern for fabric colors) and cut them out of the fabrics.

5. Trace the complete appliqué pattern onto the white rectangle cut in Step 1 (see color photo for positioning). Fuse the appliqués to the white rectangle and machine-appliqué them in place with thread that matches the appliqué fabric and a machine satin-stitch. Then narrow the satin stitch to ⅛″ and stitch the tendrils and detail lines, as you did for the apron.

Full-size appliqué patterns for the tote bag. Seam allowances are not included.

Closeup of the tote bag, showing appliqué details.

6. For the borders of the front, using the garden print fabric, cut two A strips, 3½″ × 8½″ each; stitch them to the top and bottom of the white appliquéd panel with right sides of fabric facing and ¼″ seam allowances. Cut two B strips, 3½″ × 13½″ each; stitch them to the sides of the unit in the same way (Figure 11-8). Press the tote bag front.

7. Cut one 13½″ × 14½″ piece and two 16″ × 4″ strips from the garden print fabric for the handles. Set them aside.

8. From the natural solid cut two 13½″ × 14½″ pieces for the tote lining. Stitch the lining pieces together, with right sides facing, along one long edge and both short edges, using a ¼-inch seam allowance, to make a bag shape.

9. From fleece, cut 2 13½″ × 14½″ pieces and two strips, 1″ × 16″ each. Set the strips aside for the handles.

10. Baste one 13½″ × 14½″ fleece piece to the wrong side of the appliquéd tote front and the other 13½″ × 14½″ piece to the wrong side of the same-size print piece cut in Step 7 to make the tote back. Quilt the tote front and back as you desire by hand or by machine (See the Basic Techniques chapter for quilting information.)

11. With right sides of fabric facing, stitch the tote front and back together along the bottom and side edges. Clip the corners of the seam allowances to reduce bulk.

12. Pleat the bottom of the lining bag by aligning the side seam with the bottom

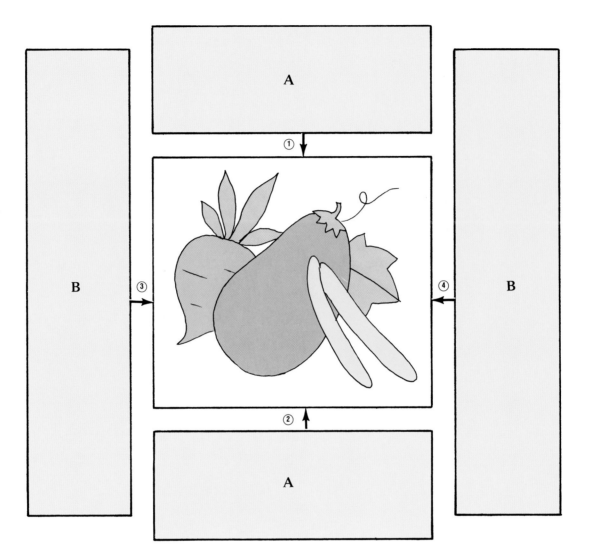

11–8. *Attaching borders to the tote front. Circled numbers indicate order of piecing.*

seam of the bag, so it forms a point. Stitch across the point exactly 1″ from the tip (Figure 11-9a). Repeat for the second corner of the lining bag. Do this on the tote outer bag as well. Turn the outer bag right-side out after pleating (Figure 11-9c).

13. To make the handles, fold under ¼″ along one long edge of each floral strip cut in Step 7 (Figure 11-10a) and press. Then place the print strips face-down on your work surface. Center the fleece strips cut in Step 9 along each fabric strip. Fold the unfolded long edge of each floral strip to the center over the fleece (Figure 11-10c). Turn the already-folded edge of each floral strip over the center of the fleece strip, enclosing the fleece and the raw edges of the first fold (Figure 11-10c). Stitch down the center fold of each handle (Figure 11-10c). Press the handles.

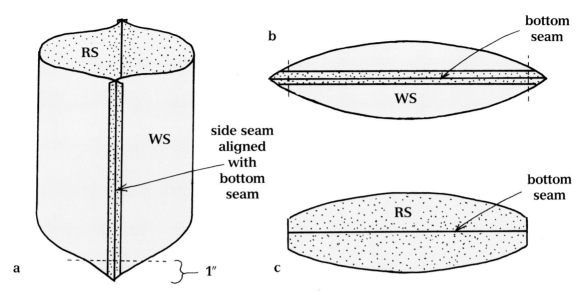

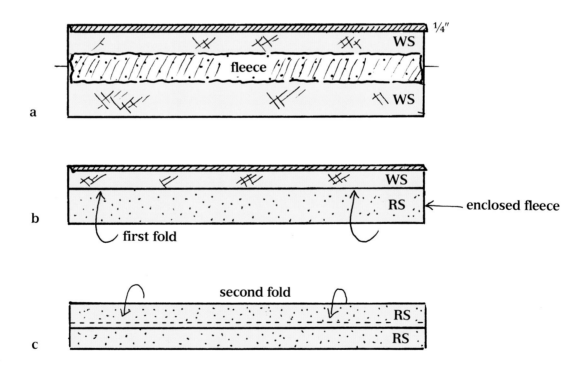

11–9. *Pleating the bottom of the bag.*
a: Stitch across the point 1″ from the tip.
b: Bottom view of bag. c: Bottom view, right side.

11–10. *Making handles. a: Fold under 1″ of strip to wrong side. Center the fleece strip on the strip. b: Fold up the unfolded strip over the fleece. c: Fold down the top edge and stitch.*

14. Baste one handle to each side of the outer bag, with the raw edges of the handles 4" in from the side seams (Figure 11-11), and aligned with the raw edges of the bag's top.

15. Place the outer bag inside the lining bag with right sides together, align the seams, and baste and stitch the bags together along the top edge with ¼" seam allowance, leaving a 6" opening in the un-appliquéd side through which to turn the bag.

16. Turn the bag right-side out. Push the lining bag into the outside bag, and press the entire bag. Sew up the remaining 6" opening. Then stitch around the top of the bag, close to the edge, to keep the layers from shifting.

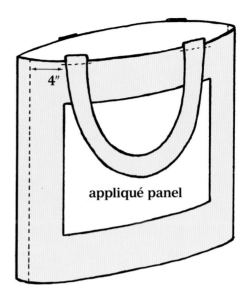

4"

appliqué panel

11–11. Baste the handles to the right side of the outer bag.

Dandelion Tea Set

You'll be sure to enjoy these weeds more at your tea table than in your yard! The bright colors will enliven even the gloomiest of days. Finished size of tea cozy: 12" high × 14" wide. Large pillow: 16" × 16". Small pillow: 12" × 12". Tablecloth: 42" × 42".

Materials Required for Set

- *2½ yards white fabric*
- *2 yards medium yellow print fabric*
- *1½ yards deep yellow solid fabric*
- *1 yard medium green print fabric*
- *⅓ yard medium green solid fabric*
- *All-purpose thread to match fabrics*
- *2 pieces of a lofty quilt batting, 13" × 15" each (for tea cozy)*
- *16" square pillow form*
- *16½" square of fleece or batting*
- *12" square pillow form*
- *12½" square of fleece or batting*
- *1 yard narrow double-fold bias binding (1" wide when opened, ¼" wide when finished)*
- *1½ yards of fusible webbing*

Directions

All seam allowances are ¼". All marking on fabric should be done with washable pen or pencil.

Tea Cozy

1. Enlarge the reduced tea-cozy pattern given on page 117 and trace it onto heavy paper or plastic. (See the Basic Techniques chapter for enlarging instructions.) From white fabric, cut one cozy shape for the front. Cut 3 cozy shapes from the medium yellow print fabric for the backing and the lining. Set them aside.

2. Trace out the appliqué patterns on page 121 onto template plastic or cardboard, label the fronts, and cut them out.

3. Trace 3 outer circles, 3 inner circles, a large leaf, a reversed large leaf, and one small leaf onto the paper side of fusible webbing and cut them out of the webbing.

4. Fuse the outer circles to the wrong side of the medium yellow print fabric; fuse the inner circles to the wrong side of the deep yellow solid fabric. Fuse the two large

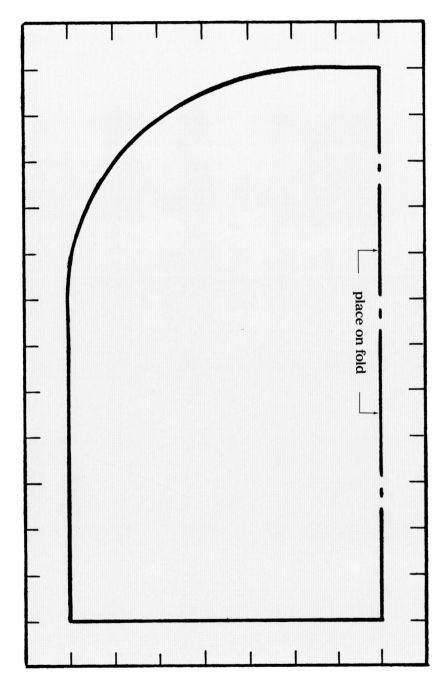

place on fold

*Reduced tea cozy half-pattern. 1 box = 1″ × 1″.
Enlarge the pattern and trace it onto folded plastic
or heavy paper.*

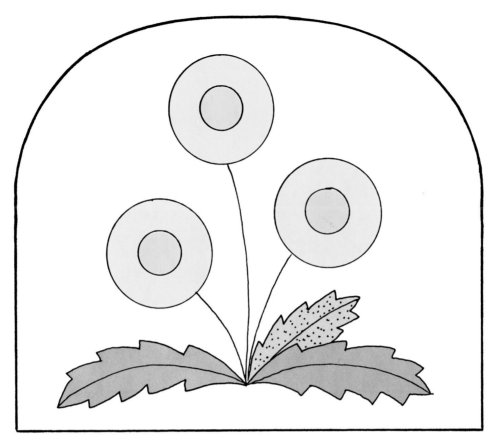

12–1. *Front of tea cozy, showing appliqué placement.*

leaves to the wrong side of the green solid fabric. Fuse the small leaf to the wrong side of the green print fabric. Cut out all the shapes.

5. Referring to Figure 12-1, fuse the appliqué shapes to the white cozy front cut in Step 1. Draw the stem lines from each flower to the center of the leaf group.

6. Machine-appliqué the pieces in place, using a medium-width machine satin stitch and threads to match each appliqué shape. Machine-embroider the stems from the flower to the leaves in satin stitch. (See the Basic Techniques chapter for appliqué details.)

7. Cut two tea cozy shapes from the 13″ × 15″ pieces of high-loft batting, using your enlarged pattern. Baste one batting piece

to the wrong side of the appliquéd tea cozy front. Quilt around the appliqué pieces by hand or machine. To quilt the dandelion effect into the flowers, thread the machine with deep yellow all-purpose thread. Straight stitch a zig-zag effect from the inner circle of the flower to ¼″ beyond the outer circle of the flower (see Figure 12-2 and the closeup photo). Set it aside.

8. Baste the second piece of high-loft fleece cut in a cozy shape to the wrong side of one of the medium yellow cozy shapes cut in Step 1. It will be the cozy back. Set it aside.

9. For the ruffle, cut two strips, 5″ × 44″ each, of the medium yellow print fabric. Fold one strip in half along its length with the right sides together. Stitch across the

Closeup showing details of machine embroidery and quilting.

short ends. Clip the corners of the seam allowances and turn the strip right-side out. Mark its center. Then gather the strip along its double raw edge (Figure 12-3a and b). Repeat this with the second yellow strip.

10. From the medium green print, cut two strips, 3″ × 44″ each. Fold each and stitch it across its short ends, and turn it right-side out, as you did for the yellow strips in Step 9. Gather the double raw edges in the same way.

11. Place the green ruffle around the right side of the tea cozy front with the center of the

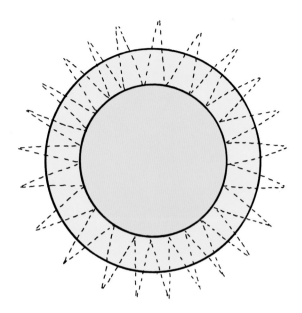

12–2. *Embroidering the dandelions. These points are very easy to machine-stitch. Start straight-stitching at the inner circle. When you have stitched ¼″ beyond the outer circle, put the machine in reverse to stitch the second side of the point back towards the inner circle. The points should be of random widths and distances from each other, and neatness* doesn't *count here.*

folded edge

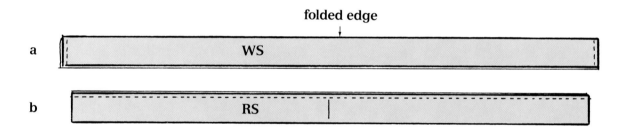

a

WS

b

RS

center

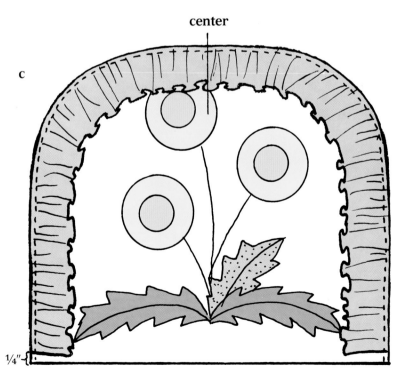

c

¼″

12–3. *Making the ruffle for the tea cozy.* **a:** *Fold each ruffle strip in half on its length and stitch its short ends.* **b:** *Turn it right-side out and gather it.* **c:** *Baste the gathered green ruffle to the tea cozy top, leaving ¼″ at the lower edge unruffled. (The yellow ruffle will be basted on top in a similar way.)*

ruffle at the top center of the cozy. The short ends of the ruffle should end ¼″ from the bottom edge of the cozy (Figure 12-3c). Baste the green ruffle in place. Then baste the yellow ruffle directly over the green ruffle.

12. To make the outer cozy, stitch the cozy front to the fleeced yellow cozy back with right sides facing and a ¼″ seam allowance. Stitch along the curved edge only; leave the straight (bottom) edge unstitched.

13. Stitch the two remaining yellow cozy shapes, cut in Step 1, together, with right sides of fabric facing. Stitch them with ¼″ seam allowance along the curved edge only, to make the cozy lining.

14. Place the outer cozy and the lining together, with wrong sides facing, and baste them together along the bottom edge.

15. Baste yellow bias binding around the bottom edge on the outside with right sides of fabric facing. Stitch it with ¼″ seam allowance to the cozy. Turn the loose long edge of the binding inside and slipstitch it in place.

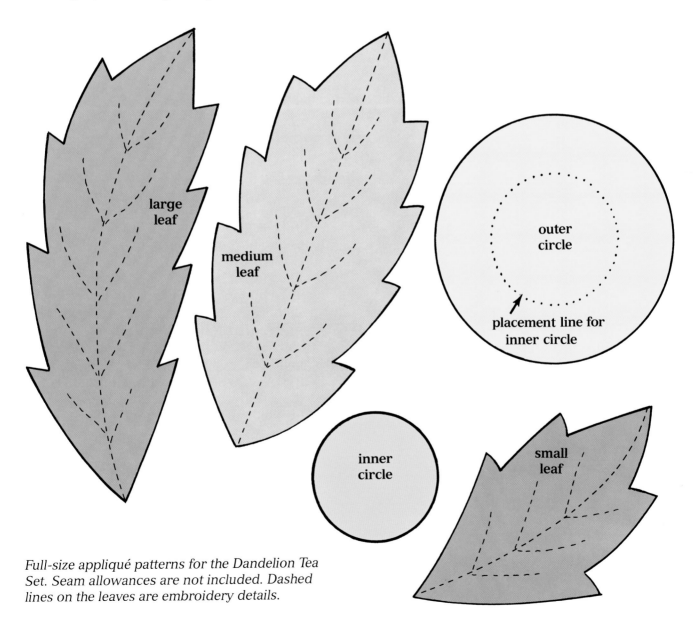

Full-size appliqué patterns for the Dandelion Tea Set. Seam allowances are not included. Dashed lines on the leaves are embroidery details.

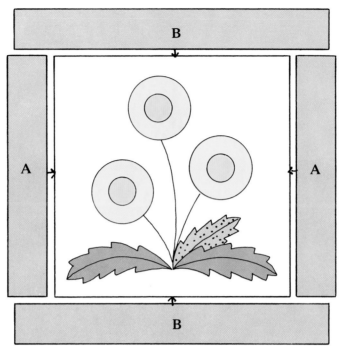

12–4. *Appliqué placement and border attachment for the 16" pillow. Attach A border strips first; then the B strips.*

16" Pillow

1. Cut a 12½" white fabric square.

2. From the appliqué pattern, trace 3 complete flowers, one large leaf, one large leaf reversed, and one small leaf onto the paper side of fusible webbing and cut them out of the webbing.

3. Fuse the shapes to the wrong sides of the proper fabrics (see the Tea Cozy instructions) and cut them out. Referring to Figure 12-4, arrange the appliqués on the white square and machine-appliqué them in place as for the cozy (see Tea Cozy appliqué instructions). Satin-stitch along the stem lines as you did for the tea cozy.

4. From the medium green print fabric, cut two A strips, 2½" × 12½" each, and two B strips, 2½" × 16½" each. Referring to Figure 12-4, stitch the borders to the appliquéd pillow panel with right sides of fabric facing and ¼" seam allowances. Press the unit.

5. Baste the 16½" × 16½" piece of fleece or batting to the wrong side of the pillow top.

Quilt the top, as you did for the tea cozy.

6. To make the ruffle, cut 4 strips of medium yellow fabric, 6½" × 40" each, and stitch them together on their short ends to form a long strip (see Figure 1-16a, p. 40). Join the outer short ends to make a circular band of cloth. Press the seam allowances open. Fold the band in half along its length with wrong sides of fabric together, so the raw edges of both sides of the band meet and the short seams are aligned. Press. Run basting stitches through both thicknesses of the band at the raw edges and gather it to fit the pillow's perimeter. Place the ruffle on the pillow front, aligning the raw edges of the ruffle with the raw edges of the pillow front, and clipping into the ¼-inch seam allowance of the ruffle at the corners. Distribute the ruffles evenly and baste the ruffle to the pillow top ¼-inch from the edges (Figure 1-16b).

7. Cut a 16½" × 16½" square from the medium yellow fabric to be the pillow back. Stitch this square to the pillow top, with right sides of fabric facing and ¼" seam allowances along 3 sides, leaving the

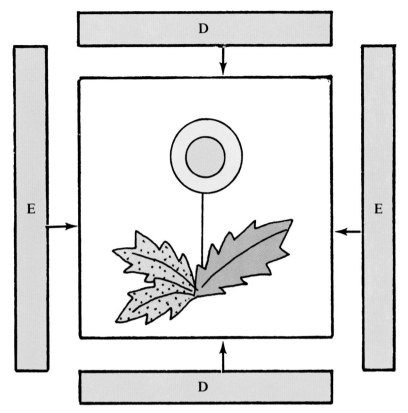

12–5. Appliqué placement and border attachment for the 12″ pillow. Attach the D strips first; then the E strips.

bottom edge open. Clip the corners of the seam allowances and turn the pillow cover right-side out. Press. Insert the pillow form and stitch the opening closed.

12″ Pillow

1. Cut an 8½″ square from the white fabric. From the appliqué pattern, trace one flower, one large and two small leaves onto the wrong side of fusible webbing and cut them out.

2. Fuse the webbing pieces to the wrong side of the proper fabrics (see the Tea Cozy instructions for fabrics) and cut them out.

3. Arrange the pieces on the white square as shown in Figure 12-5 and machine appliqué them as you did for the cozy appliqués. Satin-stitch the stem line.

4. From the deep yellow solid fabric, cut 2 D strips, 2½″ × 8½″ each, and two E strips, 2½″ × 12½″ each. Stitch them to the white center panel as borders (see Figure 12-5).

5. Baste the 12½″ piece of fleece to the wrong side of the appliquéd square. Machine-quilt it as you did for the tea cozy (see Tea Cozy instructions). This completes the pillow front.

6. From the deep yellow fabric, cut a piece of fabric 12½″ × 12½″ for the pillow back. Stitch the pillow front to the back along 3 sides, with the right sides facing, and ¼″ seam allowances; leave the bottom open. Clip the corners of the seam allowance, and turn the pillow cover right side out. Press it.

7. Insert the pillow form and stitch the opening closed by hand.

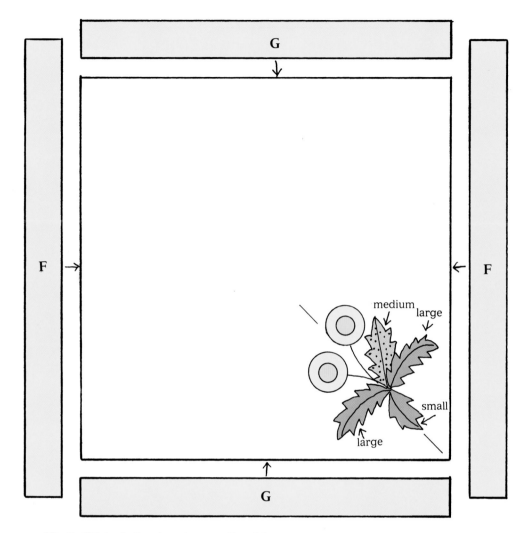

12–6. *Tablecloth, showing appliqué in one corner and border attachment. (Repeat the corner appliqué arrangement in each corner.) Attach the F borders first.*

Tablecloth

1. From the appliqué pattern, trace the following onto the paper side of fusible webbing and cut them out of the webbing. Then fuse them to the wrong side of the proper fabrics:
   4 small leaves to solid green fabric
   4 medium leaves to the medium green fabric print
   8 large leaves to solid green fabric
   8 outer circles to the medium yellow print fabric
   8 inner circles from the solid deep yellow fabric

2. Cut out the appliqué shapes.

3. Cut one 40½″ square from white fabric.

4. Fuse one set of appliqués to each corner as shown in Figure 12-6. Machine-appliqué the pieces in place as you did for the tea cozy; machine-stitch the stem lines as well (see Tea Cozy instructions for details). Stitch the flower details as for the cozy, even though you are not quilting the flowers.

4. To make the borders around the tablecloth edges, from the medium yellow print fabric cut 2 G strips, 4½″ × 40½″ each, and 2 F

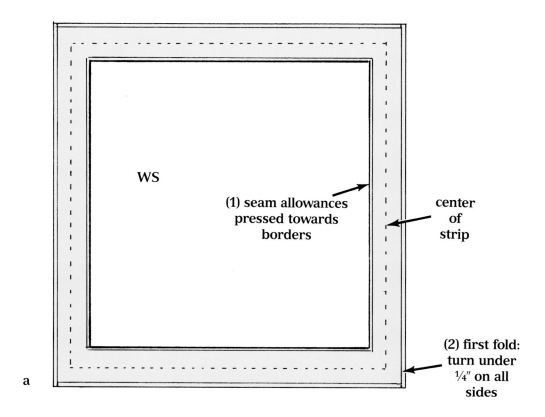

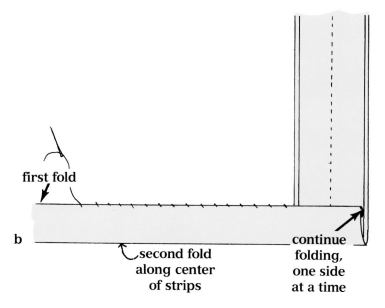

12–7. Tablecloth finishing.
a: 1: Seam allowances are pressed towards borders. 2: A ¼″ fold is made in all sides. b: The border strip is folded over the raw edges of the seam allowances where the border meets the central square, and it is hand-stitched in place.

strips, 4½″ × 48½″ each. Stitch them to the sides of the tea cloth as shown in Figure 12-6, with right sides of fabric facing and ¼″ seam allowances. Attach the F borders first.

5. Press the seam allowances towards the borders (Figure 12-7a). Press under ¼″ to the wrong side along all 4 outer edges of the tea cloth borders.

6. Fold the border strip again at the *center* of each border strip, turning it to the back of the cloth and bringing the folded edges over the raw edges of the pressed seam allowances, thus enclosing the raw edges of the seams. Hand-stitch the hem in place with matching thread. (Figure 12-7b).

Bed of Roses Quilt

The directions are for bed-size quilts, but they can easily be scaled down. A quilt using 4 blocks would make a lovely baby gift. Finished size of block: 15½″ × 15½″, including seam allowances. Finished size of quilt: Twin: 71″ × 101″; full, 88″ × 103″; queen, 96″ × 111″; king, 100″ × 115″. Number of blocks: 20 (king, queen, and full size); 15 (twin size).

Yardages of Materials Required, by Quilt Size

	Twin	Full	Queen	King
Finished sizes	71″ × 101″	88″ × 103″	96″ × 111″	100″ × 115″
Materials required				
Floral print fabric for outer borders	3¼ yds.	3½ yds.	3½ yds.	3¾ yds.
Yellow print fabric for inner borders and flower centers	3 yds.	3¼ yds.	3¼ yds.	3½ yds.
White solid fabric	1¼ yds.	2 yds.	2 yds.	2 yds.
Light green fabric	¾ yd.	1 yd.	1 yd.	1 yd.
Medium green fabric	¾ yd.	1 yd.	1 yd.	1 yd.
Scraps of at least 3 shades of pink and 3 shades of rose fabric, in total yards	1½ yds.	2 yds.	2 yds.	2 yds.
Backing fabric of choice	75″ × 105″	92″ × 107″	100″ × 115″	104″ × 119″
Quilt batting	75″ × 105″	92″ × 107″	100″ × 115″	104″ × 119″
Extra-wide double-layer bias binding	10 yds.	11 yds.	12 yds.	13 yds.

All-purpose thread to match fabrics is also required.

Directions

All piecing is done with right sides of fabric facing. All seam allowances are ¼″ throughout the project. The full, king, and queen-sized quilts all use the same quilt centers so all the steps are the same until it's time to cut the outer borders (Step 17). The twin size quilt is slightly different; modifications to the directions are given in brackets. [See Figure 13-11.]

1. From the yellow fabric cut 2 H border strips, 3½″ × 75½″ each, and two I border strips, 3½″ × 66½″ each, and set them aside. [For twin size, H is 3½″ × 75½″ and I is 3½″ × 51½″.] From the remaining yellow fabric cut twenty 3½″ squares. [For the twin size, cut 15.]

2. From the white fabric cut seventy 3⅞″ squares. Cut each square in half on the diagonal to make a total of 140 triangles. [For twin size, cut 53 squares; cut in half they will make 106 triangles.]

3. Cut 35 squares from light green fabric and 35 squares from medium green fabric, all 3⅞″ × 3⅞″; cut each square in half diagonally, as you did for the white squares, to make 140 green triangles. [For twin size, cut 27 squares of light green and 27 squares of medium green, all 3⅞″ × 3⅞″. Cut each in half diagonally to make 108 triangles. Discard one triangle of light green and one of medium green. You now have 106 triangles total.]

4. Stitch one white triangle to each green triangle for a total of 140 pieced A squares (Figure 13-1). Set them aside. [For twin size, you will have 106 A squares.]

5. From the white fabric, cut eighty 3½″ B squares and cut twenty 3½″ × 9½″ G rectangles. [For twin size, cut sixty 3½″ B squares and fifteen 3½″ × 9½″ G rectangles.]

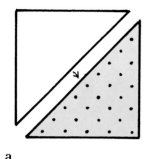

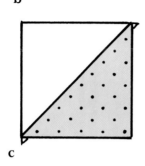

13–1. *Make pieced squares of* **(a)** *a white triangle and a green triangle, by stitching them on their diagonals* **(b)**. *Then press them open* **(c)**.

6. From the rose and pink print scraps, cut twenty 3½″ D squares and a total of 100 C and F rectangles (80 for C rectangles and 20 for F rectangles). Each C and F rectangle is 3½″ × 6½″. (See 13-2 and color photos for color planning.) [For twin size, cut 15 3½″ D squares and a total of 75 C and F rectangles (60 C rectangles and 15 F rectangles), each 3½″ × 6½″.]

Overview: Each block is made up of 5 rows. First we will piece the rows for one block, as described below (see Figure 13-2). Pink C rectangles are all of the same color within one block. D squares and F rectangles are also the same color, within a block (see color photos and Figure 13-2).

7. Referring to the Figure 13-3, assemble Row 1 from two white B squares and two pieced A squares. (Colors of green may vary here and elsewhere.)

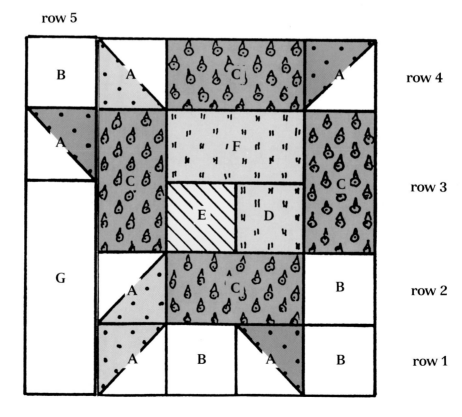

13–2. *Diagram of a pieced block, showing rows and pieces.*

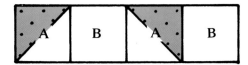

13–3. *Piecing Row 1.*

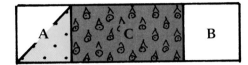

13–4. *Piecing Row 2.*

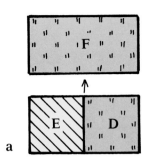

a

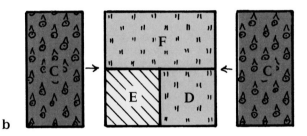

b

13–5. *Piecing Row 3.* ***a:*** *Piecing the center unit.* ***b:*** *Attaching the side rectangles.*

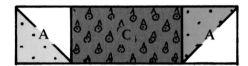

13–6. *Piecing Row 4.*

8. To make Row 2, stitch together one white B square, one rose or pink C rectangle, and one A square (Figure 13-4).

9. For the Row 3 center unit, stitch one pink D square to one yellow E square. Press. Stitch the unit to one pink F rectangle of the same pink as the D square (Figure 13-5a). [Note: in the model the position of the yellow E square was sometimes varied in Row 3 for variety.]

10. Stitch one rose C rectangle to each side of the center unit to complete Row 3 (Figure 13-5b).

11. To make row 4, stitch one A square to each end of one rose C rectangle (Figure 13-6).

12. To make the vertical Row 5, join one white G rectangle, an A square, and a white B square (Figure 13-7).

13. Press each row. Stitch the rows together to make a complete block, joining the horizontal rows first and the vertical row 5 last, with right sides of fabric facing. [Note: in the model, Row 4 was sometimes rotated for variety.]

14. Make 19 more blocks in the same way, varying the colors as desired, but always having a yellow square at the flower center (see color photo). [For twin size, make 14 more blocks.] Press each block after completing it.

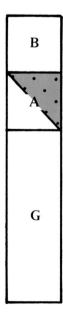

13–7. *Piecing Row 5.*

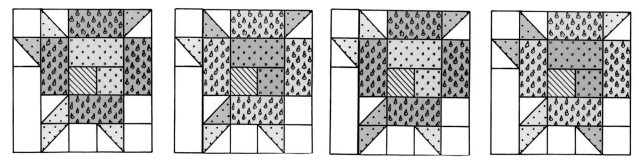

13–8. Assembling 4 blocks to make a row: king, queen, and full size. [For twin size, assemble rows of 3 blocks.]

15. The flower blocks may be rotated by you when you assemble them to provide variety in the way they are joined (see color photo). To join the flower blocks into rows, lay out the blocks in 5 rows, 4 blocks in each row [for twin size, 3 blocks in each row], on a large area such as a worktable or the floor. Position the blocks in an order and direction that is pleasing to you. Then label each block at the top with a bit of tape so you know what position it is in, what row it is in, and how it is turned (e.g., "row 4, block 2"). After that, stitch the blocks together on their sides to make rows of 4 across (see Figure 13-8) [for twin size, 3 across]. After you have made five rows of 4 blocks across, stitch the rows together on their long sides to form the quilt center (see Figure 13-9, center, for guidance.) [For twin size, see Figure 13-11.]

Borders, Quilting, and Binding

16. Stitch the yellow inner border strips, cut in Step 1, to the quilt center. First attach the I strips to the sides of the quilt center; then attach the H strips (Figure 13-9). [For twin size, see 13-11.]

17. For the queen-size outer borders, cut 2 J strips 15½" × 81½" each from the floral fabric and 2 K strips, 15½" × 96½" each, from the same fabric. Stitch them to the quilt top, attaching the J borders to the sides first; then add the K units to the top and bottom (Figure 13-10). [For the twin size, cut J strips of 10½" × 71½" each and K strips of 10½" × 81½" each. For the full size,

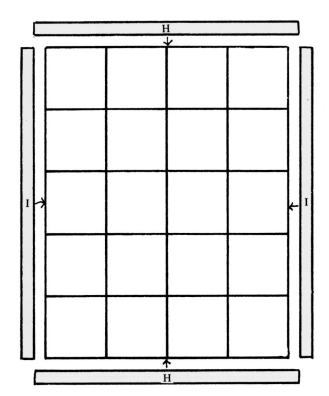

13–9. Joining the yellow inner borders to the quilt center. Attach the I borders to the sides; then the H borders.

cut J strips of 11½" × 81½" and K strips of 11½" × 88½". For the king size, cut J strips of 17½" × 81½" each and K strips of 17½" × 100½" each.]

Assemble the blocks in an order and direction that is pleasing to you.

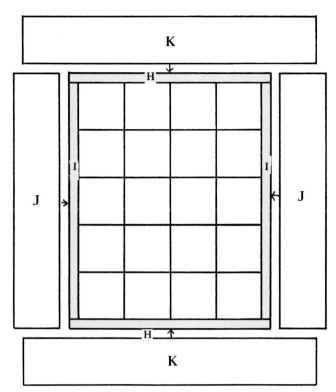

13–10. *Construction diagram for a full-size, queen-size, or king-size quilt.*

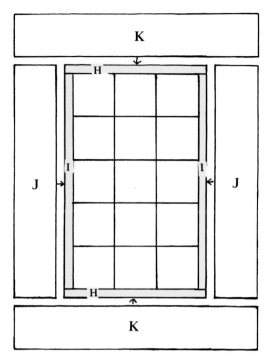

13–11. *Construction diagram for a twin-size quilt.*

strips of 11½″ × 81½″ and K strips of 11½″ × 88½″. For the king size, cut J strips of 17½″ × 81½″ each and K strips of 17½″ × 100½″ each.]

18. Place the backing fabric on a clean floor, face-down, and tape it in place. Center the batting over the backing. Center the quilt top, right-side up, over the batting and pin or hand-baste the layers together, starting at the center and working outward, smoothing the fabric as you pin. (See the

Basic Techniques chapter for basting and quilting instructions.)

19. Hand- or machine-quilt the quilt as you desire. After quilting, baste close to the raw edges around the outside of the quilt and trim away any excess batting and backing.

20. Bind the edges of the quilt with the bias binding; see the Basic Techniques chapter section on binding for further information.

Hanging a Quilted Project

To hang a wall hanging or quilt, follow the steps given below:

1. Cut a strip of fabric (it could be the same fabric as your quilt back) 8″ wide and of length 1″ shorter than the top of your wall hanging. (For example, if the top is 36″, the strip would be 8″ × 35″.)

2. Fold the strip lengthwise, with right sides together, and stitch it along the long side to form a tube. (a)

3. Turn the tube right-side out.

4. Hem each end.

5. Flatten the tube so that one long side is a fold and the other has the seamline on it (b). Press.

6. Center the tube length on the back of the quilt top center.

7. Sew the folded edge of the tube along the top of the quilt back with a hand slipstitch and strong thread (c).

8. Smooth down and attach the other long seam edge of the tube to the quilt back with slipstitching; now both long sides are attached but the ends of the tube are open.

9. Choose a dowel, rod, or flat wooden strip slightly wider than the quilt top. Put the rod or other support through the tube of material and hang the wall hanging on the wall.

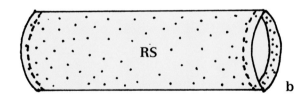

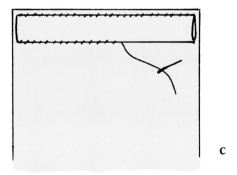

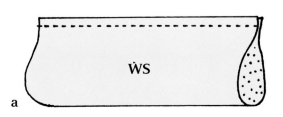

a: Form a tube. *b:* Flatten it. *c:* Attach it to the quilt back.

Quilting Patterns

Quilting pattern, Spinning Flowers. (Could be used in a solid block, if you use solid blocks in the quilt.)

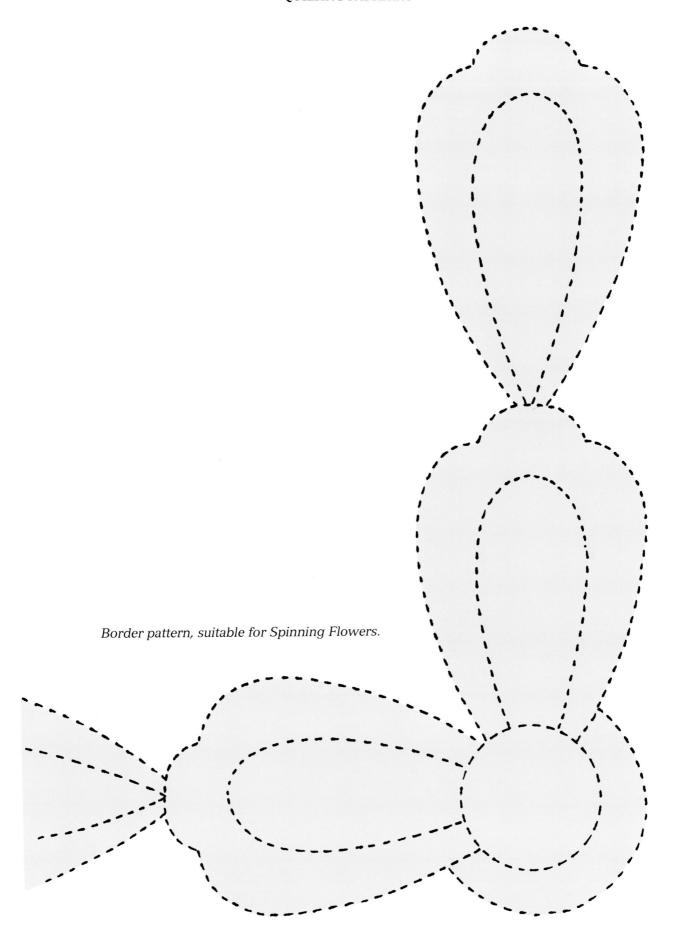

Border pattern, suitable for Spinning Flowers.

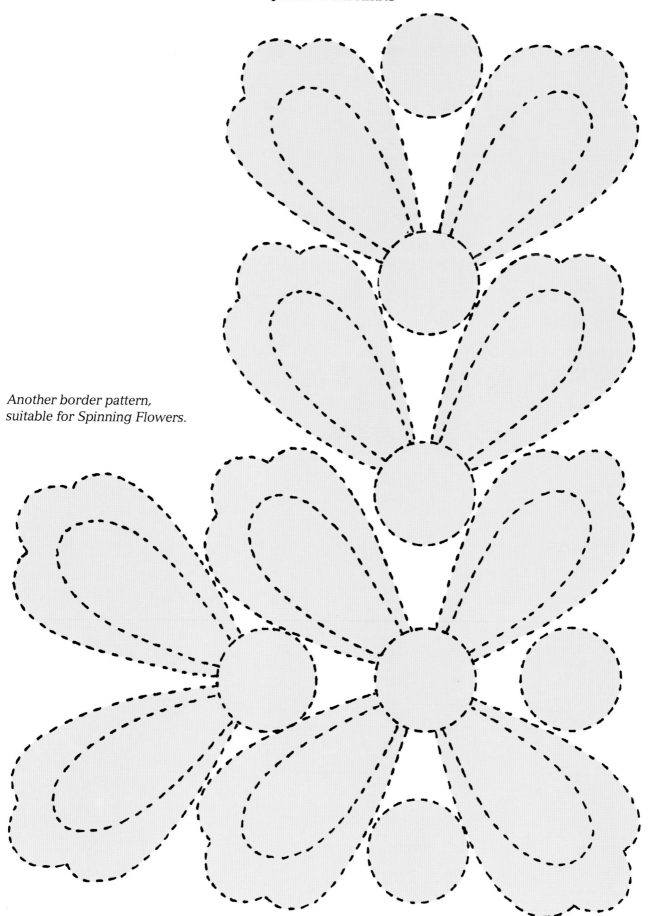

Another border pattern,
suitable for Spinning Flowers.

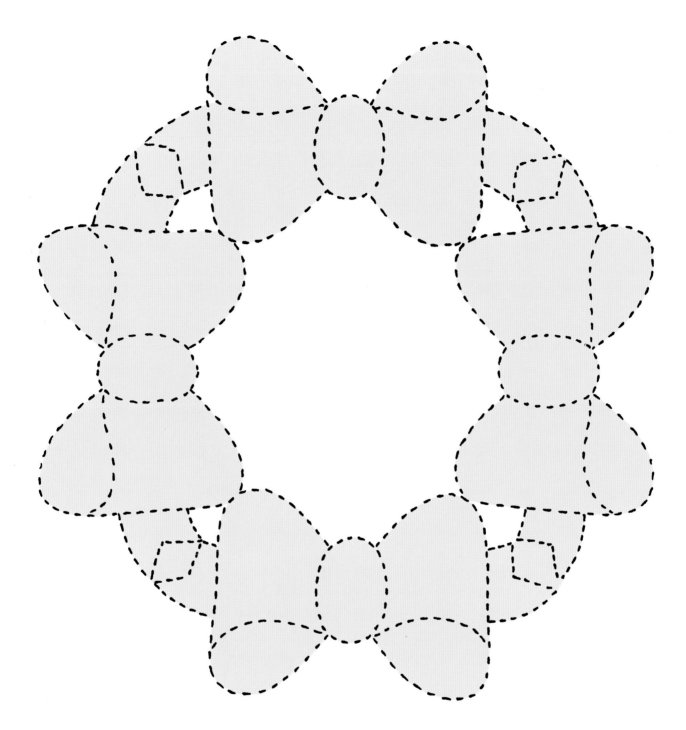

Block quilting pattern, Straw Hat Wall Quilt. (Could be used in a solid block, if you use solid blocks in the quilt.)

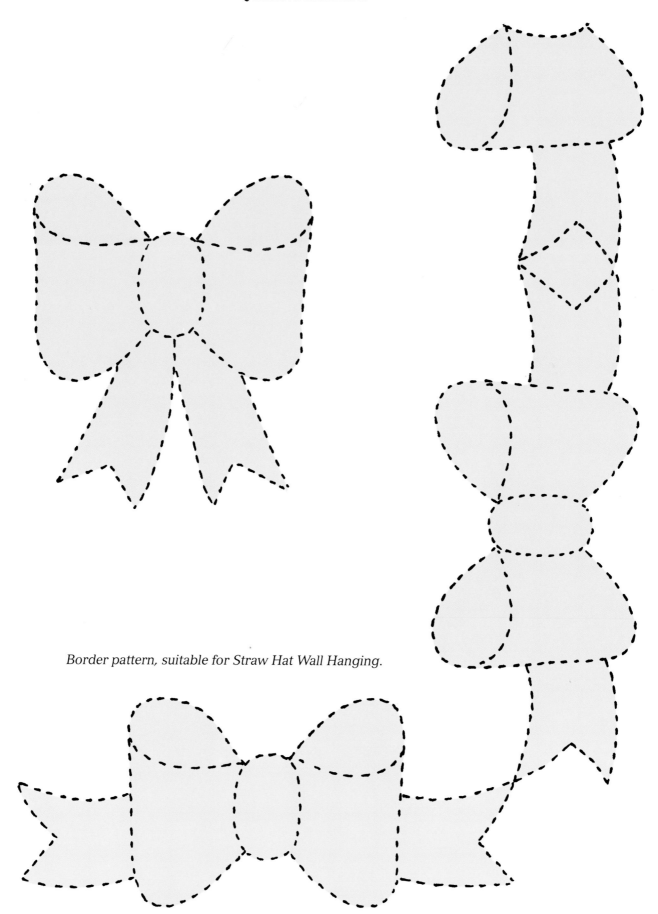

Border pattern, suitable for Straw Hat Wall Hanging.

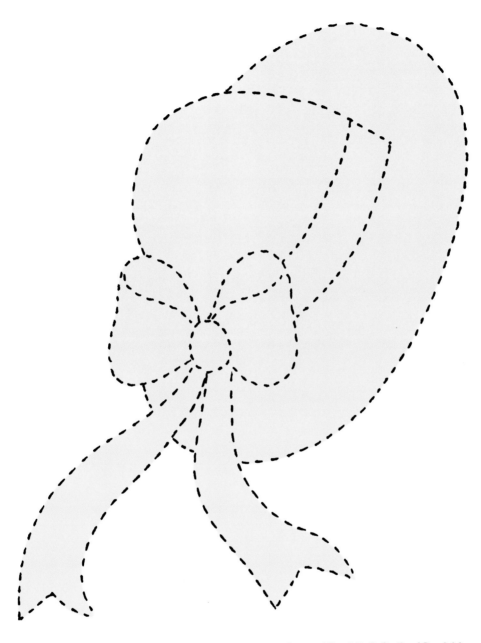

Block quilting pattern, Straw Hat Wall Quilt. (Could be used in a solid block, if you use solid blocks in the quilt.)

Useful Tables

Yardage Conversion Chart: Equivalent Available Fabric Areas for Various Fabric Widths

Fabric Width:	35″	44″–46″	50″	52″–54″	58″–60″
	Yardage Equivalents				
	$1\frac{3}{4}$	$1\frac{3}{8}$	$1\frac{1}{4}$	$1\frac{1}{8}$	1
	2	$1\frac{5}{8}$	$1\frac{1}{2}$	$1\frac{3}{8}$	$1\frac{1}{4}$
	$2\frac{1}{4}$	$1\frac{3}{4}$	$1\frac{5}{8}$	$1\frac{1}{2}$	$1\frac{3}{8}$
	$2\frac{1}{2}$	$2\frac{1}{8}$	$1\frac{3}{4}$	$1\frac{3}{4}$	$1\frac{5}{8}$
	$2\frac{7}{8}$	$2\frac{1}{4}$	2	$1\frac{7}{8}$	$1\frac{3}{4}$
	$3\frac{1}{8}$	$2\frac{1}{2}$	$2\frac{1}{4}$	2	$1\frac{7}{8}$
	$3\frac{3}{8}$	$2\frac{3}{4}$	$2\frac{3}{8}$	$2\frac{1}{4}$	2
	$3\frac{3}{4}$	$2\frac{7}{8}$	$2\frac{5}{8}$	$2\frac{3}{8}$	$2\frac{1}{4}$
	$4\frac{1}{4}$	$3\frac{1}{8}$	$2\frac{3}{4}$	$2\frac{5}{8}$	$2\frac{3}{8}$
	$4\frac{1}{2}$	$3\frac{3}{8}$	3	$2\frac{3}{4}$	$2\frac{5}{8}$
	$4\frac{3}{4}$	$3\frac{5}{8}$	$3\frac{1}{4}$	$2\frac{7}{8}$	$2\frac{3}{4}$
	5	$3\frac{7}{8}$	$3\frac{3}{8}$	$3\frac{1}{8}$	$2\frac{7}{8}$

Note: Reading across will give you equivalent areas of available fabric in various fabric widths. For example: $1\frac{3}{4}$ yards (63″) of 35″ wide material will give you 2268 in² of material; $1\frac{3}{8}$ yards (49.6 in) of 45″ wide material will give you 2232 in² of material; $1\frac{1}{4}$ yards (44″) of 50″ wide material will give you 2200 in² of material; $1\frac{1}{8}$ yards (40.5″) of 54″ wide material will give you 2187 in² of material; and 1 yard (36″) of 60″ wide material will give you 2160 in² of material; all the areas on one line across are approximately equal.

The following table is a guide for you, if you want to adapt the projects in the book to the color scheme you have in a room.

Color Harmony Table

Color	Its Complement	Related Colors
Blue	Orange	*Warm:* Blue, blue-green, green, yellow-green, yellow, orange *Cool:* Blue, blue-violet, violet, red-violet
Blue-green	Red-orange	*Warm:* Blue-green, green, yellow, yellow-orange *Cool:* Blue-green, blue, blue-violet, violet, red-violet
Blue-violet	Yellow-orange	*Warm:* Blue-violet, blue, blue-green, green, yellow-green *Cool:* Blue-violet, violet, red-violet, red
Green	Red	*Warm:* Green, yellow-green, yellow, yellow-orange *Cool:* Green, blue-green, blue, blue-violet, violet
Red	Green	*Warm:* Red, red-orange, yellow-orange, yellow, orange *Cool:* Red, red-violet, blue-violet, blue
Red-orange	Blue-green	*Warm:* Red-orange, orange, yellow-orange, yellow, yellow-green *Cool:* Red-orange, red, red-violet, violet, blue-violet
Red-violet	Yellow-green	*Warm:* Red-violet, red, red-orange, yellow-orange *Cool:* Red-violet, violet, blue-violet, blue
Orange	Blue	*Warm:* Orange, yellow-orange, yellow, yellow-green, green *Cool:* Orange (pastel), red-orange, red, red-violet, violet
Violet	Yellow	*Warm:* Violet, red-violet, red, red-orange, orange (pastel) *Cool:* Violet, red-violet, blue-violet, blue, blue-green
Yellow	Violet	*Warm:* Yellow, yellow-orange, orange, red-orange, red *Cool:* Yellow (pastel), yellow-green (pastel), green (dark), blue-green, blue
Yellow-green	Red-violet	*Warm:* Yellow-green, yellow, yellow-orange, orange *Cool:* Yellow-green (pastel), green (dark), blue-green, blue
Yellow-orange	Blue-violet	*Warm:* Yellow-orange, orange, red-orange, red *Cool:* Yellow-orange (pastel), yellow (pastel), green (dark), blue-green

Metric Equivalents:
Inches to Millimetres (mm) and
Centimetres (cm)

Inches	mm	cm	Inches	cm	Inches	cm
⅛	3	0.3	9	22.9	30	76.2
¼	6	0.6	10	25.4	31	78.7
⅜	10	1.0	11	27.9	32	81.3
½	13	1.3	12	30.5	33	83.8
⅝	16	1.6	13	33.0	34	86.4
¾	19	1.9	14	35.6	35	88.9
⅞	22	2.2	15	38.1	36	91.4
1	25	2.5	16	40.6	37	94.0
1¼	32	3.2	17	43.2	38	96.5
1½	38	3.8	18	45.7	39	99.1
1¾	44	4.4	19	48.3	40	101.6
2	51	5.1	20	50.8	41	104.1
2½	64	6.4	21	53.3	42	106.7
3	76	7.6	22	55.9	43	109.2
3½	89	8.9	23	58.4	44	111.8
4	102	10.2	24	61.0	45	114.3
4½	114	11.4	25	63.5	46	116.8
5	127	12.7	26	66.0	47	119.4
6	152	15.2	27	68.6	48	121.9
7	178	17.8	28	71.1	49	124.5
8	203	20.3	29	73.7	50	127.0

Yards Into Inches

Yards	Inches	Yards	Inches
⅛	4.5	1⅛	40.5
¼	9	1¼	45
⅜	13.5	1⅜	49.5
½	18	1½	54
⅝	22.5	1⅝	58.5
¾	27	1¾	63
⅞	31.5	1⅞	67.5
1	36	2	72

Index